P9-AEY-574

PARIS IN AMERICA

A Deaf Nanticoke Shoemaker and His Daughter

CLARA JEAN MOSLEY HALL

with
Gayle Williamson

GALLAUDET UNIVERSITY PRESS
Washington, D.C.

Gallaudet University Press
Washington, DC 20002
http://gupress.gallaudet.edu

© 2018 by Gallaudet University.
All rights reserved. Published 2018
Printed in the United States of America

ISBN: 978-1-944838-35-5

Library of Congress Cataloging-in-Publication Data

Names: Hall, Clara Jean Mosley, 1953- author. | Williamson, Gayle, 1966-
   author.
Title: Paris in America: a deaf Nanticoke shoemaker and his daughter / Clara
   Jean Mosley Hall with Gayle Williamson.
Description: Washington, DC: Gallaudet University Press, [2018] | Includes
   bibliographic references.
Identifiers: LCCN 2018032026 | ISBN 9781944838355 (pbk.) |
   ISBN 9781944838362 (e-book)
Subjects: LCSH: Hall, Clara Jean Mosley, 1953- | Nanticoke
   Indians--Delaware--Biography. | Children of deaf
   parents--Delaware--Biography. | African Americans--Delaware--Biography.
Classification: LCC E99.N14 H35 2018 | DDC 975.1004/97--dc23
LC record available at https://lccn.loc.gov/2018032026

Cover photo: Courtesy of Jeanie Mosley Hall.
For more information and photos, go to
nativeamericansofdelawarestate.com/Mitsawokett Photos/
MoseleyJamesParis.htm.

∞ This paper meets the requirements of ANSI/NISO Z39.48-1992
(Permanence of Paper).

For my husband, Howard (Seeker of Truth), and daughters, Ilea (Healing Hands) and Karelle (Spirit Dancing); the reason for everything I do. I love you with every ounce of my being.

To the memory of my extraordinary father, James Paris Mosley, who showed me the unwavering power of love.

CONTENTS

Author's Note   ix
Preface   xvii

PART 1   1
Carnage   3
Ancestry   7
What's In a Name   22
Separation   32
Hit and Run   40
Being a Man   43
She's Gone   50

PART 2   55
Life Goes On   57
Helping Out   60
Who Was That Woman?   64
The Wilsons   66
Preparation for School   69
Mud Pies   72
Work and Wait   74
The Divorce   78
Clink, Clink, Clink:
Interpreting Sounds Not So Silent and Other Things   81
Social Changes   84
Now Daddy's Leaving Too?!   89

PART 3   105
Too Big For My Britches   107
Fun Times   112
I Am More Than My Hair   116

Integration 118
Hanging Out 121
Mrs. Parker 127
Time for Change 131
She's Back 135

PART 4 137
Building Confidence 139
The Power of Support 144
College Girl 147
To College and Beyond 151
Miracles Do Come True 155
Expect the Unexpected 162
Paradise 166
The Real World 170
Another Test 172
Our Bundle of Joy 174
Jamaica Again, Really! 177
Mr. Mandela 179
The Nursing Home Blues 182
The Call 185
The Stork Strikes Again 188
Another Move 190
Where We Are Now 197

Afterword 201
Acknowledgments 205
References 209

AUTHOR'S NOTE

"There is no label such as disabled
or handicapped in Native languages."
—Linda J. Carroll, President
Intertribal Deaf Council 1998–2002

MY PURPOSE IN WRITING THIS MEMOIR IS TO DOCUMENT family history and culture: to provide a historical anchor that includes the cultures of Native Americans, African Americans, and Deaf Americans as they intersect with each other and with the broader population. By illuminating the capabilities of people who are deaf through the example of my father, James Paris Mosley, I also hope to be a support to you, the reader, in following your passion toward your dreams and goals no matter the obstacles you may face.

One of the foundations of Native American cultures is the circle. The medicine wheel is a circle of colors representing the people of the world, energy, and spiritual components, as well as the directions of the earth: north (white: representing air, animals, receiving energy, and mental capacity); east (yellow: representing fire or the sun, determines energy, spirituality, illumination, and enlightenment); south (red: representing water, plants, giving of energy, emotionality, innocence, and trust); west (black: representing the earth and physical aspects, holds energy, insight, and introspection). These are all connected to learning, balance, self, harmony, and beauty. The circle holds the world in balance. No one is above or below the circle; thus, everyone has been created equally.

If one aspect of the circle is missing, disturbed, or has been broken, problems will occur and there is discord. That is why historically in Native American cultures, people who were differently abled were not stigmatized or perceived and labeled as "disabled" or "handicapped." There were no words to indicate such. All people, hearing or deaf, were considered gifts from the Great Spirit and a part of the circle. In fact, early Native Americans believed that the stronger spirits chose to inhabit a body with, for example, deafness or blindness, and they received honor for their choice. Before the arrival of Europeans, disease and deafness were not common among Native populations, which may also explain why there are no words to represent this condition in Native languages.

High value is placed on making wise and balanced choices in relationships and interactions with one another because they affect everyone. Our individual actions have an impact on others positively or negatively. This concept is expressed in the words of Chief Seattle who was a Suquamish Tribal Chief known for accommodating the White settlers. He said, "Man does not weave this web of life. He is merely a strand of it. Whatever he does to the web, he does to himself." Therefore, in Native cultures, being deaf is merely a description, such as being short or thin. No stigma is attached to the explanation. These ideas represent long-established beliefs within Native nations. Unfortunately, not everyone within Native cultures has adhered to the traditional ways and beliefs. There are elders, however, who have stepped up to the challenge of bringing the old ways of thinking back to the present. They are preserving traditions, customs, and the way of life that revere people who are deaf because they represent the strongest, most spiritually advanced among us.

Native American deaf people from various tribes have had difficulty accessing their Native culture because of the language barrier between hearing and deaf indigenous people. This is true of any dual culture or multicultural deaf person (see, for example, Hairston and Smith, 1983; Anderson and Miller, 2004; and McCaskill et al., 2011). The National Multicultural Interpreter Project in El Paso, Texas, and the Southwest Multicultural Interpreters Network in New Mexico are helping to alleviate issues of erroneous interpreting for multicultural deaf individuals by mainstream interpreters who are not familiar with indigenous cultural differences. It is imperative that interpreters be well-versed in all languages and cultures they represent so that they can accurately convey both meaning and cultural aspects of the languages. Damara Goff Paris, one of the editors of *Step into the Circle*, the first collection of stories from Native Americans who are deaf, discusses how they come to terms with their dual identity. One writer summed it up by simply stating that he refers to himself as a Deaf American Indian when he is among people in the Deaf community where deafness and American Sign Language (ASL) form a common bond, and as an American Indian Deaf man when he is with the Native American community where Native culture is dominant.

Native Americans still experience a lack of services as well as isolation in the labor force. Certain Native populations, such as Alaska Natives, Cherokee, and Creek, have a higher rate of hearing loss due to otitis media (middle ear infections). This loss, which can lead to speech, language, and educational difficulties, can be partially attributed to the lack of access to adequate medical care, upper respiratory infections, and exposure to tobacco smoke. Some Deaf Natives have an additional barrier to deal with—the lack of access to clear and equal communication—and this has prevented them from learning about their heritage because they do not have easy access to the Elders and other spiritual leaders who could pass along cultural ways.

Historically, deaf children, like Native American children, were sent far away from their homes to schools where their heritage was not taught. Deaf Native children in American deaf schools learned ASL, which is different from American Indian Sign Language (AISL) and may not be known by hearing members of the Native Community. Karen Billie Johnson, a Diné Navajo, remembers being sent to the New Mexico School for the Deaf when she was six years old. It was the first time that she had experienced electricity and running water. While at the school, she learned ASL and the importance of pointing to identify people or objects in a conversation or dialogue. When she went back home, she learned very quickly that pointing was considered an insulting gesture in her Native culture. Needless to say, Karen had to learn how to behave appropriately in both cultures (Anderson and Miller, 2004, 30). Today, only a few Native Americans know the sign language used by Native Americans long ago, and they are just now trying to teach those who never learned.

American Indian Sign Language, which is older than American Sign Language, developed out of a need for the various tribes to communicate with each other since there were over 500 Native spoken languages used before Columbus arrived in 1492. For the Sioux, Crow, Kiowa, Arapaho, Blackfeet, Cheyenne, and others, AISL was a way to overcome the spoken language barrier, thus facilitating trade and communication during council meetings or buffalo hunts. It is not known exactly how long this system of signs had been in existence, but credit is given to the Plains Indians for perfecting its development. They were wanderers and met many other tribes as they moved from place to place, facilitating its use with a larger number of people. Before long, Europeans could see the value in learning the sign language as it afforded them better deals in trading and the knowledge that they were understood. Eventually, new signs were developed for foreign words that the Europeans used, such as "coffee" and "bacon."

Ernest Thomson Seton found AISL being used in 1882 in Western Manitoba among different Native tribes. He also noticed it being used during his travels to New Mexico and Montana in 1897. Some sign users were more proficient than others. Eton mentions one of the Sioux tribe members by the name of Sheeaka or Cyiaka (The Mudhen) living at Standing Rock in 1912. He was an expert at using AISL not only because he was Native, but also because a member of his family was deaf. He was able to sustain the use of it while other Natives who had no deaf family members were beginning to forget.

In the north, according to Wurtzburg and Campbell (1995) there is evidence of American Indian Sign Languages in existence before Europeans arrived in North America. Paris, Wood, and Miller (2002) discuss John Smoke Johnson Sakayenkwaraghton, also known as Disappearing Mist. He was a Six Nations Chief born in 1792 and made his transition in 1886. Disappearing Mist told Garrick Mallery, a nineteenth-century American Indian Sign Language expert, that tribal groups such as the Iroquois used sign language. When the Iroquois elders and warriors were present, the women and children would not use their voices as it was considered disrespectful. Instead, they would use sign language to communicate. In 1873, a delegation of Native Americans occasionally visited the Pennsylvania School for the Deaf. This is the school that my dad would eventually attend. Both groups communicated using gestures, and it was observed that Native members didn't seem to have much difficulty understanding the ASL the Deaf students and teachers were using, but the Deaf students and teachers had problems understanding the sign language used by the Native members. That may be because AISL conveys broader signs and gestures that use the larger background of the air and sky than does ASL, which tends to structure signs closer to the body. AISL conveys meanings in perhaps a more iconic way, such as the sign for "go," which is signed with an outward wave of the hand instead of the ASL sign, which uses two index fingers moving outward.

It is also known that the "people of the dawn" or "eastern people," known as Wampanoags, communicated with the first settlers using some sign language. It is possible that this Indian Sign Language may have had an influence on the sign language used at Martha's Vineyard (MVSL), a well-known signing community with a large Deaf population where everyone used sign language, whether deaf or hearing. Just as there are regional differences in ASL, the same is true for AISL. Although there may be slight changes or differences in how signs were made in various parts of the country, those differences did not appear significant enough to impede communication (Paris et. al. 2002).

Most people who are not familiar with Deaf culture and sign languages are surprised to learn that American Sign Language, used in the United States and Canada, is not universal. Just as each country has different spoken languages, the same is true for sign languages. When Americans who can hear travel abroad to a non-English-speaking country, they inevitably find someone who can speak English. In my travels abroad to places such as Australia, New Zealand, Benin, Africa, and Poland, I have found the same to be true in the Deaf community of signers. Without fail, I have always met someone who knows enough ASL for us to communicate at least on a basic level. Even if they don't know ASL and cannot understand each other's language, the facial and body grammar allows Deaf people to understand one another better than most hearing people from different countries can. Kudos to them!

Within Deaf culture, there are many famous individuals with Native American ancestry who may not be well-known among the general population. Roy Kay Holcomb (my first boss) was the director of the School for the Deaf in Delaware. His wife, Marjoriebell Stakley Holcomb (affectionately known as Mabs), was the director of the Deaf-Blind Unit, which served all children who were both deaf and blind in the state of Delaware. They both, for a time, taught at the South Dakota School for the Deaf. Dr. Holcomb was part Comanche on his mother's side. He received four master's degrees from different institutions and an honorary doctorate from Gallaudet University. His claim to fame is that he is known as the father of Total Communication, a philosophy that espoused teaching deaf children in all ways that allowed them to learn best, combining the use of speech and auditory methods, together with signing, which had been banned from use in the classroom after the 1880s. Being able to change the current view during the early 1970s of using only speech and auditory training to accepting signing again in the education of deaf children was quite a feat.

MJ Bienvenu is widely known in the Deaf community for her work in linguistics and her production of ASL media. She earned her PhD in 2003 and is a professor in the Department of ASL/Deaf Studies at Gallaudet University. Her maternal grandfather was part Cherokee and Apache.

Edith Goldston Vernon's mother was Choctaw. Edith earned a master's degree in microbiology, and minored in biochemistry. She gained national acclaim for her research in microbiology, publishing articles on the genetics of bacteria. Her additional research focused on treating tuberculosis. Edith was married to the world-renowned psychologist McCay Vernon. His research illuminated the psychological aspects of deafness. Dr. McCay Vernon was also one of my beloved professors at Western Maryland College, now known as McDaniel College.

Nathie Marbury's mother was half Navajo (Diné) and African American. Her father was African American. Nathie earned a master's degree and was the first African American woman to complete the National Leadership Training Program at California State University at Northridge.

During a very warm summer, June 14–17, 2006, my husband Howard, daughters Ilea and Karelle, and I had an incredible opportunity to attend the now defunct Intertribal Deaf Council's (IDC) 11th Conference held on the reservation in San Carlos, Arizona, and hosted by the Apache Tribe. The IDC was the first organization of Deaf Native Nations. Today, many of the members have reorganized into a new group called The Sacred Circle. The theme of the conference was "Circle of Unity: Many Cultures Woven Together to Create One Future." I had the privilege to meet so many prominent Native American Deaf people from the United States and Canada, including Elder Onalee Cooper, Dr. Howard Busby (Hatak Falaya), Damara Goff Paris (one of the editors of *Step into the Circle: The Heartbeat of American Indian, Alaska Native, and First Nations Deaf Communities*), Judy Stout, Mark Azure, Jeremy, Little Bear, Ms. Melanie McKay-Cody, and James Woodenlegs, the appointed spiritual leader for the conference. They all hold prominent positions in Native American Deaf culture.

To my surprise, I also met Teresa Norris, a Native American Deaf woman who lived in my home state of Delaware! We became like sisters during my stay. Although she was living in Delaware at the time, Teresa's heritage is from the Ojibwa tribe, found mainly in Ontario, North Dakota, Michigan, Wisconsin, and Minnesota. Delaware is home to the Nanticoke and Nanticoke Lenni-Lenape. It was such a joy to meet everyone. Prior to the conference, I had never met any other Native Americans who were also Deaf, or if I had, I didn't know it. The only Native Americans I ever knew about who were Deaf were in my immediate family.

However, on a recent visit back home, I discovered that there happens to be a man who is deaf living in the home on the Indian River built by my cousins' great-grandfather, Isaac Harmon, a famous historical figure in the Nanticoke community. Isaac, at the age of eighteen had begun to purchase back Nanticoke land a little at a time. Over the years, he had purchased somewhere between 800 and 1,000 acres. Today, his descendants and other Nanticoke live on that land.

To discover more about the Nanticoke, you may want to visit the National Museum of the American Indian, a Smithsonian Institution located in Washington, DC, or read *Delaware's Forgotten Folk* by C. A. Weslager; *The Nanticoke Indians: Past and Present* by C. A. Weslager; *A Native-American Encyclopedia: History, Culture, and Peoples* by Barry M. Pritzker; *The Indians of North America: The Nanticoke* by Frank W. Porter; and *A Vocabulary of the Nanticoke Dialect* compiled by William Vans Murray and edited by Daniel G. Brinton. You may also want to visit www.nanticoke-lenape.info, and www.nanticokeindians.org.

PREFACE

THE IDEA OF WRITING THE STORY OF MY AND MY FATHER'S life came to me at some point when I realized, after having two daughters of my own, I was perpetuating the same pattern that had occurred years before my birth. No one in my family could go back through their genealogical tree any farther than their grandparents. My daughters, Ilea and Karelle, did not have the opportunity to grow up with and know my parents or grandparents except through the few stories that my husband and I shared with them. Initially this book was for them.

In 2000, I began the James Paris Mosley Scholarship Foundation Fund with the Cleveland Foundation in Cleveland, Ohio, to honor my father's memory and to financially support Deaf students with their college goals. During the writing of this book, it became evident that his life would not only be an inspiration to my daughters, but also to the many culturally diverse Deaf students that could appreciate a strong Deaf role model.

To anyone who wants to live their best life, this story is also for you. It is my hope that as you read this memoir, you will be inspired to develop your own dreams and create goals, and that you will keep working on them one day at a time until you succeed.

People have often said to me, "Your life is a fairy tale. Things come so easily to you. Goldie Roberts, one of my friends, jokingly said once after a conversation we had about some of the activities my daughters were involved with, "When I come back in another life, I want to come back as one of your kids."

Yes, there have been many wonderful opportunities that have come my way; however, not without difficulties that all of us experience in life. What I have learned, though, is that your past does not have to dictate your future. If you want something out of life, you have to put something into it. If you do, life will unfold for you in a way that you could never have imagined. If you can conceive of a dream, believe that it can happen, and are willing to put the work in, then it will happen. It could even be better than you could have ever expected. I have found that life is much like the final scenes in Steven Spielberg and George Lucas's movie *Indiana Jones and the Last Crusade*. Indiana, played by Harrison Ford, must take a leap of faith to get from one side of a mountain to the side of a different mountain. He, at first, doesn't see a way to bridge the vast divide. There is nothing but huge space and a significant drop between him and his destination. If he steps out, he will surely perish into oblivion. Nevertheless, he closes his eyes and steps out into nothingness. As he does so, a long wooden board sprinkled with golden dust magically appears under his feet to guide him over to the other side. Sometimes we just have to trust that the multiverse will provide exactly what we need at just the right time we need it, not one moment sooner.

The major part of this memoir takes place in the great state of Delaware where I was born. It is also the birthplace of my family. Delaware is a gem of a little state that has much to offer. It's only a couple of hours drive long from top to bottom and geographically speaking, is the second smallest state in the nation right behind Rhode Island. I grew up in sleepy Dover, Delaware, the state capital, which sits in Kent County, the middle of Delaware's three counties: New Castle, Kent, and Sussex. I was the only child of a Deaf shoemaker and his Deaf wife, who left us both when I was very young. By the time I was in my tumultuous teen years, I felt like nobody expected me to do much, and for a long time I believed that my only option was to grow up and take my place among Dover's adult Black citizenry, most of whom were firmly entrenched in the lower to middle classes. Life in Dover was good if that was all you knew.

I left when I was in my twenties and did not go back for any significant amount of time after that. I still have family there who I talk with and visit with as much as my time allows, but in general, I haven't spent much time there. It took a long time before I would come to see it as part of my emotional life. A lot of things happened there that I've wanted to leave behind. But a lot of good has come with me from there, too. You don't hear much about Delaware, good or bad. It is one of those states people tend to forget about when they are trying to name all fifty states. They get to forty-seven and then have to be reminded of North and South Dakota and Delaware. Historically, though, it has an interesting personality.

During slavery, it separated free states from slave states. Although, quiet as it's kept, Delaware was a slave state (at least that was true of the southern third). The Mason-Dixon Line runs just under Sussex County, so that on paper Delaware looks like a Free State. The southernmost county of Sussex was slaveholding while the northern counties of Kent and New Castle were not. Eventually, segregation packed its bags and moved on with a bit of an attitude.

Its proximity to Pennsylvania, specifically Philadelphia, has given Delaware a distinctly northeastern spin as well. Much of our media comes out of Philly. And, lacking a sports team of our own, we tend to root for the Eagles, the Phillies, and the Seventy-Sixers.

We have some distinctly southern traditions as well. We drink our tea sweet, and southern hospitality runs pretty strong through the neighborhoods. When I was growing up, most people left their doors unlocked. Entering in and out of each other's homes required only a knock on the door, which was immediately answered with a "come on in!" Family members and friends came in and out on almost a daily basis. It was like each friend or family member's home was an extension of your own. Peaches, scrapple, and succotash were mealtime staples. People from Delaware speak with an accent. I didn't realize that until I had been gone for quite some time. When I would phone someone that lived in Delaware, I noticed that they all had a similar character to their voice. This pattern of speech was different from people in other parts of the country. My husband and daughters would tell me that as soon as I began speaking on the phone with a relative from Delaware, I would slip into the same accent. I had no clue I was doing that!

There was also a lot of green space. Mennonite and Amish communities surrounded Dover, along with a number of independent farms. The horse and buggy was as common a sight as a car traveling down one of Dover's main thoroughfares, Forest Street, which was also the street I grew up on. The Amish and Mennonites came into town to shop, get their shoes fixed, or deliver eggs, cheese, and vegetables to shopkeepers.

Unlike the larger urban city of Wilmington with its skyline and tall buildings, Dover did not have a building more than three or four stories high and those were usually the state office buildings or the buildings at what was then called Delaware State College, now known as Delaware State University.

For entertainment, we went to the Capitol Theater, the one theater in town. Back then, Black folks were not permitted to sit downstairs, but were relegated to the balcony. Frankly, the view was better from up there, but that was a secret we kept to ourselves. The theater closed in the Eighties and, after extensive renovations, reopened in 2001 as the Schwartz Center for the Arts.

One summer, I went back home as a side trip to a larger trip my family took and I got a chance to go back to the Schwartz Center (née Capitol Theater) for a film festival. It was the summer of 2010 and Dover was showing its southern hospitality. The trees bloomed in bright colors, a gentle breeze moved in from the east, the sun was warm, and the sky was the kind of blue you only see in paintings. The day was everything I loved about living in Dover. I had come to view the work of a young African American filmmaker and graduate of Delaware State University.

I had left Dover more than thirty years previously, eager to get my life started, without much regard for what I was leaving behind. I came back periodically with the same attitude. Dover was simply the place where I grew up. I didn't know what I would think upon entering the old Capitol Theater. I hadn't given it much thought, not really. The last time I had been there was when I was a little girl and had to sit in the balcony. I didn't think that it ever really bothered me that I sat there because I'd had to. To be honest, I never even thought I'd think about it like that. To this day, when I go to the movie theater, I will go as far up the stairs and toward the back as possible. It gives you a broader view of everything on the screen.

When I opened the doors and went into the theater, I walked in on freshly varnished floors, expanded space, and new seats, but it was still the Capitol Theater. When I took my seat at the orchestra level, the formerly restricted level, amid the opulence of the now renovated theater, I felt my breath catch and my eyes began to sting. I didn't break down in a full sob, but the magnitude of the moment hit me harder than I thought it might. Surprisingly, as my eyes began to tear, my husband Howard asked me, "what's wrong?"

I told him, "I didn't expect to have this reaction."

If someone had asked me the day before, I would have told them it was just a theater, a place to see the local movies. I had my friends and my family and the balcony was as good a place as any to sit. I would have admitted to no emotional reaction to Jim Crow laws or segregation. It just was. But here I was, doing what my father had never been able to do in his lifetime, what I had not been able to do my entire childhood, and what my daughters could now take for granted.

Dover had changed.

I realized, so had I. This was not my first trip back to Dover, but I was here now to be with family. I was no longer the girl whose parents were Deaf, whose mother had left, and who everyone had expected to just grow up and take the prefab slot that had been cut especially for her in Dover.

In writing this memoir, I have written events as I remember them. Others may remember them differently. I have changed some names and identifying details to protect the privacy of individuals. It is my hope that in reading these pages, you will not only learn about my and my father's life together, but that you will be inspired to live your dream and be able to see how you too can overcome and defeat obstacles that will inevitably appear in your life.

If you have the attitude that everything that happens to you is for the greater good, even if it sometimes comes disguised as failure, defeat, wrong turns, and just plain old crap, you will be happier and able to enjoy life so much more while you are getting through the tough times. I am still learning these lessons. We have to go through our own trials on our own trail to get to our triumphs. What I have also learned is that if you are patient and can give yourself time to get through it—not giving up, continuing to do the work necessary, giving it your best, all with a positive attitude—there is sunshine and joy on the other side. These are the times when you can learn the most about yourself. These are the times that will propel you to become your greatest self!

PART 1

.

Carnage

SOMETHING HAPPENED IN THE SPRING OF 1983 THAT threw me into complete inner turmoil. I was thirty and had been married to my husband Howard for five years. I had just given birth to our highly anticipated first child, Ilea. I was at home asleep on a late night in State College, Pennsylvania, home of Pennsylvania State University, where my husband and I were faculty members. Howard was an assistant professor in the Department of Psychology and I was an instructor in the Communication Disorders Department.

This was a night like any other until the phone rang and Mommom, my Daddy's older sister—who was also known by her other nieces and nephews as Aunt Lib—called from Dover. She always called me from time to time, but this time her voice sounded strained and trailed up at the end as if she were checking to see if it was really me on the other end of the line.

"Jeanie?"

"Oh, hi Mommom. How are you?"

There was silence; she didn't answer the question.

Then after what seemed an eternity, she blurted out, "Your daddy has been attacked in his own home and he looks bad, real bad!" She seemed to struggle to keep from going into complete hysteria.

Mommom was the matriarch of our family. She always reminded me of Queen Elizabeth II. They shared the same name. Physically they looked alike in body type and facial features, although Mommom's skin was more of an olive complexion. She even wore her hair in a similar style . . . without the hats. When she dressed up to go to Whatcoat Methodist Church, her shoes and pocketbook always matched.

She was always the strong one that everyone else looked to in times of trouble, but the quiver in her voice let me know that she was having a

My Uncle Pick, Mommom, Charles, Dad, Aunt Grace, and my grandfather Wingate leaning on my dad's car.

tough time holding it all together. I sat up straight. "What do you mean, what happened?!" I screamed back at the receiver.

My heart sank as my stomach churned. I thought I knew Dover. I had grown up in Dover, after all. I had wandered the streets by myself and with other friends at all hours of the day and night and had never come to any harm. Dover wasn't without its issues, but people generally felt safe there.

I never liked the idea of leaving Daddy alone, but my reasons were mostly personal. His safety was always a concern, but it didn't really occur to me that somebody in Dover would do what they did to him. It's a perspective-changing event.

After this, it was impossible for me to see Dover with the same innocence. I had no idea that kind of evil worked under the surface and that was an uncomfortable thought.

Whoever had attacked him must have been watching the house. Our house in Dover was a very small bungalow that my dad and his father built together by hand. It had a living room, kitchen, two bedrooms, a bathroom located between the two bedrooms, and a front and back porch. The very thought of someone spying on our home sends chills up my spine. It was like something out of a Hollywood thriller, part of the paranoia of American life. But that buffer that separates us from the hapless victim in the film, that safe feeling of being able to walk away from the movie theater and say "That could never be me," had been dissolved.

I grew up in the era of *the neighborhood*. Eyes were always watching, but instead of meaning harm, they were there making sure you were doing what you were supposed to be doing, not watching and waiting to steal from or harm you. The one thing I thought anybody in Dover should be paranoid about was getting caught doing the *wrong* thing.

Dover's a smaller town. Whoever it was that attacked him probably knew Daddy was deaf, alone, and vulnerable. Lately, he had been having balance issues, not uncommon among deaf people. He would walk in a pattern that resembled a person who had too much to drink. It is estimated that as many as 30 percent of deaf people have difficulty with balance because the systems of balance and hearing are both located inside the inner ear. If something goes haywire with one of those systems, it can cause problems with the other. In particular, but not exclusively, it affects those who became deaf from Type 1 Usher's Syndrome, which includes both hearing and vision loss, as well as those who became deaf from meningitis. Daddy's deafness stemmed from scarlet fever.

Daddy's assailants probably sat waiting to take advantage of a man who could not help himself. Sometimes the things people are capable of unnerves me.

As far as we could tell, someone broke into the house, entered the living room from the front porch, and beat him—a sixty-eight-year-old man of medium build with just a touch of gray in his black hair—to a pulp. Daddy was probably sitting in his favorite chair, a metal lawn chair with green and white plastic woven strips, in front of the TV. Blood was spewed and spackled all over the living room sofa, the off-pink wall, and everything on it. I used to sit on that old sofa to watch my favorite TV shows like *I Dream of Jeannie*. After the assailant(s) left, Daddy, beaten, bloody, and bruised, crawled inch by inch a half a mile on his hands and knees to his sister's—Mommom's—house. To get there, he had to crawl across a very busy street, cross an expansive lawn that always had a huge growling dog chained up to a tree with a very long leash ready to attack any trespassers, and then go down another side street until he reached the end of the block where his sister lived. Only God knows how many hours it must have taken him to complete that lengthy trek in his condition. After all of that, he had just enough strength left to climb up her front steps and bang on the aluminum part of her storm door, which must have sounded like hailstones hitting a tin roof. He couldn't hear the sound he was making, but he certainly understood the power that sound had on people who could hear.

When Mommom and her husband Norman Manuel Durham—affectionately known by many as Pick, perhaps because he was very slim like a toothpick in his younger days—came to the door to see what the commotion was all about, they found Daddy collapsed on their front lawn.

Later, when I first saw the living room where Daddy had been beaten, it pained me to think of how much he must have suffered. Daddy was never able to identify who did it. We always assumed they were looking for money or things they could sell, perhaps for drugs. Maybe they just wanted to beat up an elderly deaf man. Daddy could never discern a motive and neither could the police. As far as we could tell, nothing was missing from the home. They probably thought since Daddy was deaf, he wouldn't be able to tell anyone what happened.

I now have come to grips with this event and see the perpetrator(s) also as a victim—a victim of their environment. They were a part of an ever-growing reality in our society of violence that we have yet to solve.

Ancestry

BEFORE WE GET TO WHAT HAPPENED NEXT, I THINK IT IS important to share with you some background information to help you understand my dad and how he and others impacted me. My life journey began before I was ever born. I like to think of it like that because I believe that everything I do and everything that was done before I got here somehow leaves a mark. And so my journey began even centuries before I arrived on this planet, and all that came before is imprinted on me somehow, and that I will make my imprint on it in some way.

This life that I live is not totally mine. It is part of the lives of my ancestors and the lives of my descendants. I am as much a part of the past as I am the future. It is my responsibility then, to not run from, but rather to cherish the past and shape the future.

I didn't always know that.

My mother was born deaf from no known cause on January 4, 1928, near Cheswold, Delaware (this is how the location is actually listed on her birth certificate). She was a beautiful, slight, African American woman with some Native blood. Everyone else in her family could hear. Her family was from Marydel, a small town on the border of Maryland and Delaware, close to Dover. Her father, Benjamin Preston Simmons, Sr., was a big and tall gentleman with caramel skin. He had a deep, resonant voice that on first impression could scare the living daylights out of you, but he was as cuddly and gentle as a teddy bear. His parents were Mary Elizabeth Denby Simmons, who had Irish blood, and William Oscar Simmons, who was part Native American, although we don't know the specific tribe.

Her mother, Agnes Sudler Simmons, was a thin woman with a deep chocolate complexion. Her demeanor and voice was as soft as her husband's was thunderous. Agnes's parents were Gertrude Sudler and Thomas Henry Sudler. Thomas had a mix of African American and Native

American ancestry. According to family lore, his mother—my great-great grandmother—was Lenni-Lenape. My mother's sister, Alice, who had more of the body frame and complexion of her father and a personality to match, remembers that Thomas had an out-of-the-ordinary middle name—Catch-Me-Not.* He also had beautiful straight hair that he wore in braids. Alice and my mother remembers watching him brush his teeth using ashes (a strange enough custom, but his teeth were brilliantly white and strong).

Agnes and Benjamin had four children: my mother, who was their firstborn; Alice Elizabeth; Benjamin Preston, Jr. (Benny), who was tall and thin with the chocolate complexion of his mother; and William Oscar, whom we called Ricky. Ricky was thin, shorter than Benny, and had the caramel complexion of his father. As a young man, Ricky enlisted in the armed forces and was killed in Italy at the very young age of twenty-one in a car accident. He and three of his friends were on their way to get pizza when the car slid off a rain-slick road at night. He had been thrown from the backseat of a passenger car. Everyone else in the car survived. The family of course was devastated! I was about seventeen or eighteen years old then and close to Ricky in age, so his death was particularly painful for me.

Early in my mother's life, my maternal grandparents moved away from Dover to Clairton, PA, near Pittsburgh, so that she could attend the Western Pennsylvania School for the Deaf. At that time, it was their only option for educating their daughter.

During the summers, after my mother grew up and was on her own, my grandparents would bring my half-brother Tad, my mother's oldest son who was born when I was about three years old, to Dover. He had been left in their care. Aunt Alice and her husband Herbert Thomas, who also lived in Clairton, would bring their five girls too. Not having any siblings of my own to grow up with, I always wondered what it would be like to have a sister or brother and how it was for them to have each other for company. Birthdays meant instant parties. Anyone else invited was just icing on the cake.

Everyone seemed to get along and enjoyed each other's company. The older girls would help their parents look after the younger ones. Together,

* Within the cultures of people of color, complexion can range from very pale to very dark. It is common to include descriptions of skin color when characterizing someone. It was important to whites during the establishment of Jim Crow laws in 1887 through the 1950s to classify individuals of color for the purpose of racial segregation.

we used to hang out and pick cherries from my Great Aunt Emma and Uncle Melvin Wilson's huge backyard cherry tree. Ricky would say, "Here's a bunch over here."

"I want to get the ones way up top," I would reply.

"You'll need a ladder for those so let's just get the ones we can reach," he said. Being a few years older than me, he had better judgment.

Aunt Emma was a short, round, brown-skinned woman who was my grandmother Agnes's sister. She was a great cook, but she especially loved to bake pies and cakes. Her cherry pies and orange cakes were my favorite. Aunt Emma and Uncle Melvin never had any children, so their home was not what we would call child proof. There were many knickknacks on shelves and crocheted doilies on the backs and arms of furniture. They also had a huge, old fashioned upright piano that no one played. I would always enjoy tinkering with the keys on that old piano and dreamed I would be able to play it one day. I never did learn how. There was no extra money for lessons.

My grandmother and Aunt Emma's other sister, Evelyn Winchester, lived on the opposite side of the same street as Aunt Emma (Queen Street), but a few houses down and across a major street (Division Street). She was slighter of build and was just a bit lighter shade of brown than Aunt Emma. Aunt Evelyn had one son that was already a grown man when I was a child. He never came around that often as I recall and I never met her husband, Mr. Winchester. Perhaps he died at a young age. Perhaps they just didn't get along. Perhaps he wasn't her husband. What Aunt Evelyn was famous for was her white potato pies. Many people have heard of sweet potato pie, but you haven't tasted anything until you have tried a well-made white potato pie. Everyone said Aunt Evelyn's were the best!

When I was a very young child, Aunt Evelyn was my babysitter while my parents worked: Daddy in his shoe repair shop and my mother pressing dry cleaning at Capital Cleaners Laundry. Instead of daycare centers like we have today, parents relied on family members in the neighborhood. Aunt Evelyn not only took care of me, but also several other neighborhood children as well. There was one girl in particular I remember: Diane Driggus. She lived a few houses down from Aunt Evelyn; she and I would play together and formed a close bond. We remained friends through grade school. She has since passed away, but will always be remembered as one of my first friends.

We would all be dropped off at Aunt Evelyn's home in the mornings and then picked up after our parent got off work in the evenings. While at her home, we would watch TV shows like *Romper Room* and *Captain Kangaroo*. I don't remember too much else happening there besides watching TV and eating lunch. I can't even remember what types of food we ate. I just remember eating.

Aunt Emma's husband died while I was very young, leaving her alone to now bake for family and friends. Later, when I was in my early twenties, my grandmother would suffer the same fate.

My grandfather, Benjamin, was at home in Clairton working on his car, located on a steep incline beside his house. (If you've ever been to the Pittsburgh area, you know how steep the hills can be. I have been in a car going down one of those hills and have had to ask the driver to let me out so that I could walk because I was afraid of the car toppling over. That is pretty steep!)

Behind the house there was a vertical drop. My grandfather was under the hood with his back to the vertical drop with the car slanting away from him. Suddenly, something went terribly wrong! The car lunged forward and rolled down the embankment with my grandfather pinned under it. By the time the ambulance arrived, it was too late. My grandfather passed away on June 11, 1977.

The first time I had been to my grandparents' home that I can recall, was to attend my grandfather's funeral. Aunt Evelyn and Aunt Emma had never learned to drive, so their brother, who lived in Wilmington, drove the entire trip. I did not know him very well as he lived in a different city and was not around that often. When we arrived at my grandparents' home, oddly enough, the house was about the same size and had a similar floor plan pretty much like my own home—a bathroom between a couple of bedrooms and a kitchen opposite the living room. There must have been a sale on this blueprint.

I don't have any recollection for some reason of actually being at the funeral, but I do recall that other family members and friends had come to the home to pay their respects. Coming from Dover, maybe we were not able to arrive in time for the service, but I'm sure it was a wonderful home going celebration for my grandfather. We made a return trip the same day! I helped do some of the driving on the way back home.

My father's side of the family is from the Nanticoke Indian Tribe, one of the original inhabitants of Maryland and Delaware. They were but one of many tribes that populated Turtle Island, a name used by Native Americans referring to North America and lands that were eventually settled by Europeans. Other tribes include the Lenni-Lenape, who also lived in the area of the Chesapeake Bay and up through the Delaware River and Bay, who now live throughout Delaware, New Jersey, Pennsylvania, Ohio, New York, Maryland, and Canada.

There was quite a bit of intermarrying between the Nanticoke and Lenni-Lenape tribes in order to preserve their culture and to maintain some sense of cohesiveness against the encroaching Europeans. Some, however, decided to exchange nuptials with Whites, and some with Blacks. Many of today's decedents are a blend of all these cultures, who now live in various parts of Pennsylvania, New Jersey, Delaware, Ohio, as well as other parts of the country. The Nanticokes had two reservations in Sussex County, Delaware, the Broad Creek Reservation in Laurel and the Indian River Reservation in Millsboro. The Nanticokes also had a reservation located in Vienna, Maryland, called the Chicone Reservation. The Nanticoke Lenni-Lenape Tribe were families from the Brotherton Reservation located in New Jersey. They were historically part of a larger Lenni-Lenape tribal nation. Another branch of this Lenni-Lenape nation is living in Cheswold, Kent County, Delaware. They are the Lenape Indian Tribe of Delaware.

The original language that was spoken by the Nanticoke is part of the Algonquian family of languages used by many tribes such as the Pocomoke, Piscataway, and Choptank. The translation of the word *Nanticoke* means "Tidewater People." A few words of the Nanticoke Language such as *wohacki* ("man"), *acquahique* ("woman"), *nowoze* ("father"), *nicque* ("mother"), *nucks-quah* ("son"), *hun tawn* ("daughter"), *a-a-meh* ("yes"), and *mattah* ("no"), were recorded in 1792 by Dr. Daniel Garrison Brinton; however, the syntax used is still unclear.

The few Nanticoke that remained in Delaware during the latter 1800s settled in Indian River Hundred, bought land, and assimilated into the local culture. They purchased land, which today includes private family property; the Nanticoke Indian Center; the Nanticoke Indian Museum, which opened in 1984, and sixteen acres of land that was donated to the tribe by Hudson and Schell, LLC.

The Nanticoke have had a relationship with the State of Delaware since March 10, 1881, when they were then known as the Incorporated Body. This was a forerunner to today's Nanticoke Indian Association, Inc., established as a nonprofit in 1921 in Millsboro, Delaware. However, in 2016, legal state recognition occurred with the support of my youngest daughter, Karelle. She assisted our tribe's first female chief, Natosha Norwood Carmine, in obtaining legal counsel and was instrumental in conducting research necessary to formalize legal recognition. Today, there are approximately 1,000 Nanticoke Native Americans that live in southern Sussex County and in other parts of the state and country.

Because the skin color of the Nanticoke ranged from pale to dark, they were often mistakenly or purposefully identified as being mulattos. During Jim Crow, Whites became fanatical with skin color and began to view the Nanticoke as a special classification of colored people, similar to the categorization of those of mixed race called "coloured" in South Africa. The ambiguous identity of the Nanticoke and Nanticoke/Lenni-Lenape tribes followed them through history. Because of the current efforts to educate the public about just who we are, by holding powwows, naming ceremonies, and participating in other community cultural events, this perception is changing.

There is another pocket of Nanticoke/Lenni-Lenape Native Americans who reside in a small town called Cheswold (remember my mothers' birthplace was near this town), just a few miles north of Dover. We had relatives who lived there also. I remember visiting Cheswold more often as it was geographically much closer, about ten minutes north of Dover than Millsboro, which is considered to be the tribe's home and is where the majority of Nanticokes live. It is about a forty-five-minute drive south of Dover.

When Mommom's husband, Uncle Pick, who was Nanticoke/Lenni-Lenape, passed away March 31, 1990, we held his funeral in Cheswold. There were just a few side streets and dirt roads, and from what I remember, there may have been one traffic light.

The Nanticoke/Lenni-Lenape have a saying on their tribal flag: "We Are All Family." It's the truth.

When I was growing up, I had committed to memory the snickers, side comments, and overall view from many in the Black community that "these people"—also known by some as "Moors"—were "more" Black than White. Although there was a strong cohesiveness as a tribe among those Nanticoke who lived in the Millsboro area, that cohesiveness did not extend to those Nanticoke and Nanticoke/Lenni-Lenape Native Americans who lived in Dover among the Black community or those who lived in Cheswold or in Bridgeton, NJ. In fact, historically, there was more of a separatist feeling as far as being a tribe between these groups even though we were all family and members of the same tribes.

Separateness, I think, describes much of what my dad felt most of the time. Separate from other Natives, separate from people who could hear, and separate from the larger Deaf community in the nearby cities. When I lived at home with Daddy, he had four other Deaf friends a bit younger than him that were from around the Dover area—three African Americans: Mr. Smike, Mr. Smike's brother Jimmy, and a friend of my mother's named Helen, and a red-headed White guy named Jack. Later, there was a young African American Deaf boy, about three years younger than me who I didn't have much association with.

Daddy did not seem to be a major part of either world, African American or Native American, because of the language barrier. Except

Mr. Smike with my dad.

for the few Deaf friends he had, he just kept to himself mostly. When Mr. Smike or Jimmy came over to our home or to the shoe shop, Daddy became more animated and alive. It was as if they could make Daddy remember the fun times they shared at school. Maybe it was just because he had other adult friends he could talk with.

Mr. Smike had a hearing stepson who was my age and in my grade at school. It's funny, but we never really discussed having Deaf parents. Perhaps at that age we just didn't view it as a topic that we needed to discuss. It was what it was. Or maybe it was because Mr. Smike was hard of hearing. Although he used ASL, he could function with greater ease in the hearing world without an interpreter. When I would see him at public functions, he didn't sign to me like he would when he came to visit us at our home. He just talked.

Growing up in Dover in the 1950s and 1960s, there were no organized powwows or tribal rituals promoting Native pride that we participated in during the late 1970s. It was difficult at that time to identify with your Native heritage if you did not live in Millsboro and was not accepted by Nanticokes who were direct descendants of the original signers of the 1881 agreement between that particular group of Nanticokes and the state of Delaware. Being an individual of color, yet looking different from other Black people with whom you shared a community, promoted this kind of attitude. In high school, I remember being in some of the same classes with Nanticoke/Lenni-Lenape students who were probably my cousins. Yet, on official forms, they would check the box that indicated they were "White" or "Other," and I would check the box that said "Black."

Times have changed since then. Starting in 1977, the Nanticoke hold annual powwows, a celebration of families and friends coming together sharing culture and heritage with other tribes and non-Natives. There are ceremonial dances where dancers wear Native regalia, drumming, singing, and vendor booths selling Native American food, such as Indian tacos and succotash (a mixture of corn and lima beans in a buttery broth) and goods. The Nanticoke powwow occurs every September on the weekend after Labor Day in Millsboro, Delaware. Over the years, it has become a famous Delaware tourist destination.

In addition, the Nanticoke/Lenni-Lenape two-day powwow is celebrated every year during the month of June in Bridgeton, New Jersey, with approximately 5,000 to 10,000 visitors. Many of the powwow dances have been borrowed from other tribes, but the Toe Dance is thought to be uniquely Nanticoke. It is a traditional woman's dance to honor the Elders. It is called the Toe Dance because as the women perform, the heels of their feet never touch the ground. At the 2013 powwow, I had the amazing opportunity to see the Toe Dance. It's a very delicate dance and deceivingly difficult to do. At first glance, it appears effortless. However, upon trying to practice it outside the formal dance circle, I found it very difficult to stand on the tips of my toes for any length of time, much less walk and spin with that posture. It requires great dexterity and stamina. Today, I am able to dance inside the circle and have strengthened my toes quite a bit.

In 2011, the tribes began working to become more unified. The Confederation of Sovereign Nanticoke-Lenape Tribes, the three tribes coming together at the 2011 Millsboro powwow, demonstrated that effort. At that powwow, Chief Tommy Robbins, chief at that time of the Nanticoke in Millsboro, Delaware; Chief Dennis Coker, chief of the

Karelle and dancers at a powwow.

Lenape of Delaware; and Chief Mark Gould, chief of the Nanticoke/
Lenni-Lenape of New Jersey came together for the first time. I feel
so privileged to have had the opportunity to attend and witness this
historical event. To see the three chiefs come together as one body gives
hope to all of us that the separateness of the past will no longer be a
shadow over the tribes. As the R&B singer Frankie Beverly says, "We
are one." Let us forge the future together; there is strength and longevity
in numbers.

Today, the culture of the Nanticoke centers around teaching the
young people and others our Nanticoke heritage and past traditions.
The Nanticoke tribe has participated in various activities throughout the
state of Delaware to educate the public about our traditions. Chief Tee
Norwood and his wife Jean, both of whom have passed on, began a
scholarship fund in 2005 for Nanticoke high school students interested
in pursuing a college degree. They were also instrumental in having
the history and many artifacts of the Nanticoke people included in the

Sterling Street. (L to R) Kim Robbins, Michele Wright, Pastor Karen Mumford,
Lillian Morris, and me (front).

Smithsonian Museum of the American Indian in Washington, DC. The Indian Mission United Methodist Church, the Nanticoke Indian Center, and the Nanticoke Indian Museum serve as gathering places for folks to come together, to celebrate, and to learn. At the museum, you will find many Nanticoke artifacts and photographs of Nanticoke students who attended the Haskell Indian Boarding School in Kansas. In recent times, one of the last known speakers of the Anishinabe language, a sister language to the Nanticoke language, living in Canada, was invited to come to the Nanticoke Museum for a workshop to teach others.

Just for the record, my paternal great-grandmother was Lydia Ann Wright Jackson, born February 2, 1848, in Sussex County, Delaware. She was the daughter of Phillip S. Wright and Hannah Johnson. She was also the sister of one of the original signers of the 1881 declaration documenting the recognition of the Nanticoke by the state of Delaware. At some point prior to 1870, Lydia married Robert Jackson, who was born to Wesley Jackson and his wife Elizabeth on February 15, 1842, in Sussex County, Delaware. Robert was a seaman who worked on cargo ships and later became a farmer. One of their twelve children was my grandmother (whom I was named after) Clara Frances Jackson Mosley, born August 11, 1888, in Sussex County, Delaware. Clara was born the second to last of their children. My grandmother, Clara Frances, married my grandfather, Wingate Burton Mosley, on June 4, 1908. My great-grandmother, Lydia Ann, passed away on May 3, 1901. My great-grandfather Robert lived another fourteen years and, at the age of seventy-three, followed her in death from pneumonia on December 29, 1915. They both are buried at Indian Mission Church (formerly known as Johnson's Chapel) a historical site in Millsboro, Delaware.

My paternal grandmother Clara passed away on October 20, 1937.

My paternal grandfather, Wingate Burton Mosley, was born June 30, 1882, to Purnell P. Mosley and Eliza Jane Johnson. My grandfather Wingate passed away on January 4, 1954, ten months after I was born. Wingate and Clara are buried at Fork Branch Cemetery, near Cheswold, Delaware, another historical site where descendants of Nanticoke and Lenape tribes are interred.

Our Native American ancestry was not something my family spent a lot of time talking about. Growing up, I heard a few stories and saw

My great-grandmother Lydia.

a rare book first published in 1943 that circulated among my father's family members titled *Delaware's Forgotten Folk: The Story of the Moors and Nanticokes* by C. A. Weslager. I remember my father and aunts showing me pictures of particular relatives in the book like Perry Hughes and stories about who they were and the things they did with them.

   In another book, *A Photographic Survey of the Indian River Community*, compiled by the Nanticoke Indian Heritage Project in 1977, are also pictures of relatives. One in particular captured my attention. It was the only picture I had ever seen of my great-grandmother, Lydia Ann Wright Jackson. When I first saw it, I immediately thought how strikingly similar she and her granddaughter, my Aunt Jeannette looked. They both had straight dark hair parted down the middle and pulled back. I remember as a young child going to Indian Mission United Methodist Church in

Millsboro, Delaware, on occasion to the services, especially homecoming, and then to the after service picnics on the grounds of the church with Mommom and Uncle Pick.

Uncle Pick was a very laid back sort of guy who didn't let much bother him. He always let Mommom handle most things. He had a very fair complexion and straight black hair, which became a beautiful silky white over the years. He had a bit of what he called Uncle Arthur (arthritis) in one of his knees or hip, which made him limp just a bit when he walked, only it wasn't really a limp. It looked more like he had swag when he walked. He was cool!

Uncle Pick used to work for NeHi Bottling Company, a corporation that produced sodas in every flavor. We never had to worry about what to drink as he would bring cases of the sweet nectar home for us to drink and share with family and friends. At the Indian Mission Church picnics, there was always so much food to eat. The mild breezes whispering through the trees, along with us children being able to run around playing games of tag, made the time after church so much fun.

Aunt Sally, one of my paternal grandmother's sisters who was very light in skin tone like my grandmother, was there along with her husband, Perry Hughes, along with a host of other relatives such as her brother, Levin Jackson, a tall and slender man with an olive complexion and his wife, Caroline Coker.

At these events, I had a sense of being a part of a different group, but it was not the outward identification with Native American culture and pride that is more evident today and more closely associated with those tribes that currently live on reservations. It wasn't until later after my college years in the 1970s that I began going to the first powwows, a long overdue tradition that, as I stated earlier, the Nanticoke revived. It was much later that I began to gain an understanding of just who the Nanticoke and Lenni-Lenape people were. As far as I was concerned, I was a simple, African American girl with some Native Ancestry.

I remember Daddy being a part of just a few of these gatherings. He usually was the only Deaf person there unless Roma, Aunt Jeanette's daughter who was also Deaf, was in attendance. That was not often since she lived in Wilmington. Roma has more of the olive complexion of her mother while her sister Rita and brother Ronnie have slightly more caramel and chocolate tones, a mixture of their mother and father, Uncle

Smitty (his last name was Smith). All three were very slim, trim, and beautiful. In fact, Rita did a bit of fashion modeling in her younger years.

Early on, no one else in the family knew ASL fluently except Daddy, Roma, and me. Ronnie and Rita knew some signs that they could use to communicate what they needed to. This was not unusual during my father's generation. Today, many more people learn American Sign Language, but back then it was not viewed as a true language in the same way it is today. How isolated he must have felt not being comfortable to participate to a larger degree.

At family gatherings, family members had their own way of communicating with him using gestures, home signs (made-up signs only known to family members), and mouthing words for him to lip-read (contrary to popular belief, a challenge for many deaf people), but they could never be able to convey anything of great depth. As a young child, I often tired of having to convey everything that was going on around me. I just wanted to play. Daddy, I think, knew that and spared me from being in that predicament many times. He would only ask me what was being said if it seemed really important. Or I would use my judgment to tell him what was said if I thought it was important. As a great many deaf people have experienced, he too was the sufferer of the proverbial "never mind" or "I'll tell you later," which never comes.

Being the only one who could communicate well with my dad, I now feel terrible that, at certain times, I just didn't want to be the link between him and everyone else. I've since learned from other Children of Deaf Adults (Codas) around my age that they felt similarly at a time when there were no professional interpreters or technology available that could assist with communication.

It's difficult to be responsible for communication for your parents at such a young age. Like most Codas, I could sign before I could talk. Because Codas were able to bridge the divide between their Deaf parents and the hearing world, Deaf parents seemed to see us as little miracle workers who could solve any problem because we could hear. The fact that we, just like other children, had to go through the cognitive developmental stages seemed to get lost in the day-to-day encounters we were expected to help navigate. Children's brains are wired to handle certain levels of input as they grow. Sometimes, the information we needed to interpret was over our heads or should have been out of bounds.

Thankfully, today that responsibility is now shared with professional interpreters and technology, giving a respite to signing Codas. Codas today have a much easier time. Since the inception of the Registry of Interpreters for the Deaf (RID) in 1964 at Ball State in Muncie, Indiana, professional interpreters—not just family members or any untrained people who happen to know sign language—are now available to professionally interpret and culturally mediate the conversations between Deaf and hearing people. This ensures that everyone can understand equally and not feel discriminated against because they do not hear.

What's In a Name

IN 1915, THE YEAR MY FATHER WAS BORN, WORLD WAR I had been going on for a year (although the United States would not formally enter the war for two more years), African Americans were being lynched at an alarming rate, but they were also full of hope, jazz and the blues were taking root, women were demanding their rights, and social dancing was becoming all the craze. African Americans were in the middle of their second Great Migration from the South, trying desperately to be Americans against a strong wave of resistance.

In the face of rapid change and shifting geographies, Dad's arrival on this earth seven years after the marriage of his parents, Clara Frances Jackson Mosley and Wingate Burton Mosley on June 4, 1908, was pretty uneventful. On June 9, 1915, Dad joined his half-sister Anna Gertrude, whom we called Gertrude, born September 16, 1907; Sara Elizabeth, who was called Lib by her friends, born February 23, 1912; and Jessie Leola, born March 4, 1913. Later they all would be joined by Jeannette Frances, born January 28, 1917; a brother named Walter Warren, whom we called Warren, born January 19, 1923; and Grace Robeda, born November 5, 1925. As you can see, the middle name was an important moniker in my family. Even I prefer to be called Jeanie as opposed to my given name of Clara Jean.

There were three other births, but they did not survive infancy. Dorothy, birth date unknown. Joseph was born December 23, 1910, but passed away on March 7, 1911, just three months after being on this earth. And Henry Jackson, born June 17, 1921, who only lived four months, passing away on October 18, 1921.

Aunt Gertrude looked like her mother Clara. She was fair and seemed very tall because she towered over everyone else. In reality, everyone else was fairly short to average in height. Aunt Gertrude was 5'7" and had a laugh that was as big as she seemed tall. She seemed to always be smiling, but sometimes that smile took on a mischievous grin. All the other sisters were about 5'4", give or take an inch. They took after their father Wingate, who was shorter than his wife Clara. In their younger years, all the girls had long beautiful dark hair, olive complexions, and bodies that could have graced any of today's glamour magazines. As they got older, that changed a bit as what occurs with all of us.

My grandmother Clara.

Aunt Jessie, who was also deaf, died at the very young age of twenty-four from cancer. She also had a condition known as mastoiditis, an inflammation of the mastoid caused by an infection in the middle ear. The mastoid is a conical protrusion located on the temporal bone behind the outer ear. I never got to hear much about her, but from her pictures, she too was very attractive.

Uncle Warren was of slight build and had an olive complexion and dark wavy hair. His body, fragile from repeated seizures caused by epilepsy, still allowed him to play and have fun with his siblings in their childhood years. There were pictures of Uncle Warren in his younger days in the company of females, but he never married. During that time, if you had epilepsy, you were viewed as having a handicap. The general public saw epilepsy as a serious and life-threatening condition where individuals could not live autonomously. Today, individuals with epilepsy can live full independent lives because of the many effective antiepileptic medications. For Uncle Warren, however, the current thinking did not occur soon enough. It was believed that he could not have a "normal" existence with this infirmity, so he lived out the rest of his life in the home of his sister Elizabeth and her husband Pick after all his siblings had grown up and started their own lives. Uncle Warren passed away on March 10, 1975, at the age of fifty-two, the same year I graduated from college. After all those years being on no effective preventative medications, his final epileptic seizure was too much for his worn out, frail body to handle.

Daddy was of average height, about 5'9", and his ruddier complexion was more in line with his father's. He also had a handsome head of hair that was dark and wavy.

Mommom was the more serious sister with her "I'm not havin' it" attitude! Although she did enjoy socializing with her friends, she didn't partake of much alcohol, but did enjoy her cigarettes until she quit in her senior years.

Aunt Jeannette and Aunt Grace were the social girls who didn't mind having a drink or two. They also enjoyed their cigarettes and the company of "gentlemen callers."

The first family home of Clara and Wingate was on Railroad Avenue, named aptly because it was near the railroad tracks. The house was modest, but the noise and promise of the trains and their movement was unavoidable and undeniable. Trains would storm through the neighborhood

My grandmother, Clara, holding my Aunt Grace, and other family members and friends.

at all hours of the day and night carrying things and people everywhere and back again.

Life on Railroad Avenue did not mimic the pace of the times. It moved, instead, at a steady pace for my grandparents and their children, despite the shifting, changing world that rumbled through on the trains. Things in Dover, Delaware, went on pretty much as they always had.

My grandparents were hardworking laborers who raised their family the best they could with what they had. Although they knew they were American Indian, they never labeled themselves as such to the outside world. They had assimilated over time into Dover's Black community, like many of the Nanticoke Indians of that region, and they let people think whatever they wanted about their ethnic heritage.

The Nanticoke were small in number and, since they were not White, they had few options in where they could live. Their choices were to live in the small area of Millsboro and its surrounding region in the southern part of the state, the tiny area of Cheswold, or to integrate themselves in the neighborhoods where African Americans lived. They certainly could not live in the White neighborhoods, unless they could "pass" for White, which some in my family could do.

This reminds me of an occurrence when I was then dating my future husband, Howard, who had come to visit me. He and I were sitting on my front porch rocking in our outdoor metal and mesh rocking chairs when I noticed my Uncle Pick drive up to the package store, which is what we called the liquor store. I yelled out with enthusiasm to Uncle Pick from across the street, "Hi Uncle Pick!"

Howard then turns around to me (remember this is during the late Civil Rights era of the 1960s) and asked in all seriousness, "Why are you calling that White man your uncle?" I emphatically replied, "that's no White man. That **is** my uncle!" Howard, looking quite puzzled, just shook his head, without further response.

As an adult, my Aunt Jeannette lived in an Italian neighborhood in Wilmington, next door to Mr. Guido, a jolly, round-faced Italian man who lived alone. I used to love visiting her because she lived a few houses down from the corner store that sold the best Italian Ice ever! We didn't have such a sweet treat like this at any of the shops in Dover.

My grandfather Wingate (called Wink-it) was known around Black Dover as "Shorty Fender" because he was short and had a car with a beat-up fender. Dover could be like that. The nicknames one received could be considered endearments given by friends.

My grandparents worked many jobs. They believed in the American work ethic: If you work hard, you can achieve. He was a farmer by trade, but at night he worked on the railroad, paving and inspecting the tracks. He also worked as a maintenance man at Delaware State College before the name was changed to Delaware State University. My grandmother cleaned state government buildings and worked the farm. They always had food on the table and their six surviving children got the best education they could afford, which is to say they went to public school.

Content as they were, they were not without their little dramas, though. They were subject to the same indignities as other people of color in the south. On my Aunt Grace's birth certificate, she is listed as "collard." It is unclear if they thought she was a leafy vegetable or if they believed she was "colored." Either way, they were mistaken.

My father's birth certificate and various other vital statistics are no less a casualty of bureaucratic indifference. According to his birth certificate, my father's name is Parris Mosley, born June 9, 1915. His real name—the name given to him by his parents—is James Paris Mosley, although they always called him Paris. Someone, either at The Bureau of Vital Statistics in Delaware or Mary Mosley the midwife, didn't get it quite right when they recorded his name. Later, his original school enrollment forms would reveal that he was born the same month and day, but a different year, 1914. His school records also have his mother's name and his name listed incorrectly and declares that he was born deaf, which was also incorrect. Such was life for the Mosley's.

My family existed on the railroad tracks not worrying about the way other people's lives were changing and how those changes might affect them. They had their own worries. The renaissance belonged to the Black elite, something my grandparents and their family had no relationship with. The rest of the people got on with the business of feeding their families and trying to live in a hostile world. They were not creating the art, but they were its subject.

The waterlogged bureaucracy that had renamed my father and added a year to his life became simply an anecdote in the family history we trot out when we need something interesting to say. But still . . .

Our names tell the world that we are here, and what it expects of us, as well as what we expect of it. Naming a child is the most important thing parents can do. I suspect that my grandparents chose their children's names carefully, just like any other parent. The process often begins early and doesn't end until their wishes are inked in stone on the birth certificate. The child then becomes a living, breathing symbol of their expectations. My grandparents, I'm sure, were no different.

Around the same time Wingate and Clara were marking my father's arrival in this world, in New York, Cleveland, Detroit, and a whole host of other places, cities were winding up for the renaissance of blackness that would forever put Black art on the map of the world. Those train tracks my grandfather inspected and repaired recorded the movement, and my family could feel it rumbling under their feet and rattling under their skin whenever the trains rolled by. They might not even have understood how rapidly their world was changing, or had any concerns about the renaissance that was taking shape under their very noses. They were Native Americans who had assimilated into the Black culture out of necessity. Their lives ran parallel to the Black community without truly intersecting. They lived and worked among Black people and took the social lumps heaped on them by those who didn't bother to differentiate (not that it would have mattered if they had). My guess is if you asked them about the Harlem Renaissance, they wouldn't have an inkling of what you were talking about, but the movement went through them anyway because they lived on the railroad tracks that went through Dover.

Other things rumbled through Dover and across the country without the aid of railroad tracks. The influenza epidemic, also known as the Spanish flu, hit Delaware officially in September 1918, but all records indicate that it had probably already been there a while. The flu missed my family, which at its peak, killed between 20 and 50 million people, more than was killed in World War I.

We weren't so lucky with scarlet fever. In the summer of 1918, scarlet fever came to my grandparents' home. Today scarlet fever is no big deal, a heightened version of strep throat, an inconvenience at best. The doctor prescribes an antibiotic and things get back to normal pretty quickly. But in the 1910s, things weren't quite so simple or easily resolved. Antibiotics wouldn't be discovered for another decade. And for poor Blacks and assimilated Native Americans, a doctor was hard to get. Scarlet fever ran its course and the patient took his chances.

In the Mosley house, my father was the one whose hearing chance took. There are conflicting stories as to exactly when and how my father contracted the virus. Mommom says he was about six months old. My father said he was about 3 years old. Nobody even hazards a guess as to who was right or how it happened. According to all accounts, though, he developed an extremely high fever, which is one of the leading symptoms of scarlet fever; one estimate had it at about 106°.

I tend to think my father was closer to right on that one. Three seems like a more viable age for him to have survived the sickness and for it to take his hearing. If he had been six months old, I wonder if he would have even endured such a high temperature. His speech would also not have developed as much as it did. My father could detect high frequencies and he still had some small remnant of speech available to him. In order to have maintained that level of speech, he may have had some access to it before he lost it, but there is no way to know for sure.

So, around 1918, my father had contracted scarlet fever and because of it, lost his hearing. No one remembers how the family discovered my father could no longer hear. There are no stories of trying to talk to him where he didn't answer back or making loud noises to find out he couldn't respond. Any of these scenarios might be true, but neither of them has ever been offered as part of the family lore.

My father's hearing loss never seemed to be an issue to his family. It just was. It did not seem to be a source of shame, and they didn't seem to offer him any pity for what a lot of people consider a disability. Perhaps it was that Native American perspective of not viewing the differently abled as "handicapped." It was only important that he couldn't hear and they figured it out. The more exciting thing to them (and justifiably so) was that he had survived scarlet fever.

His parents expected of the deaf James Paris Mosley the same thing they expected of the hearing James Paris Mosley. Because of the way their schedules worked, everyone, including my father, was required to pull his and her own weight by helping to cook, clean, and do other basic household chores. My grandmother Clara was a strict disciplinarian.

I am sure the family was disheartened at this new wrinkle in his development, but the fact that there is no moment to mark the occasion says a lot about the people and their expectations of life. It speaks volumes about their resolve and faith. In Native Cultures, children with a difference are considered gifts from God. It was the lot they'd been dealt and deal with it they would and did.

They learned to communicate with him by pointing and using invented gestures and having him read their lips. Hearing is such an important thing to people who can hear. For those who can hear, we assume that people who are Deaf—either by birth or from an injury—are "missing" something. In fact, many in the Deaf community who have never heard before have very little concern for what they can't hear. Theirs is a life based on vision. Beauty is in the *eye* of the beholder. People who are deaf, however, are very much aware of the impact sound has on those who can hear.

My father grew up in Dover playing and interacting with his siblings like any other child. Games like Old Maid, Cowboys and Indians, Hopscotch, Needle in the Haystack, and Stick Frog (a game that involved great dexterity and challenge at flipping a knife into the ground from different levels of height on the body) were all a part of their childhood experience.

They picked peaches, strawberries, and a host of other vegetables in the family backyard garden. There were no stories about my father being left out of any of this. No tales about his loneliness at watching the other

Dad and his siblings.

kids play while he sat on the porch. According to my aunts, my father loved to have fun and he got into his share of trouble as well.

For his birthday one year, my grandparents got him a BB gun. Dad was so excited he took it outside every day and practiced his aim shooting at tin cans and the like. One day, his sister Elizabeth came out to play. It's not clear whether she came to play specifically with him or if she was just out there playing by herself. Whatever the case, he shot the BB gun and accidentally hit Elizabeth's finger.

"What's the matter with you?! You hit my finger!!!" she screamed.

The look on his face showed his horror at what he had done. Her screams brought one of the neighbors running. The neighbor vehemently scolded my dad with a shaking of their finger.

"Bad boy!!!" they shouted while confiscating the BB gun.

Young Paris, with his head bowed, slowly walked back into the house sulking and wondering what would be his fate at the hands of his mother Clara. My father never saw that BB gun again. This was during an era where it was okay for neighbors to discipline another's child if it was warranted. This is often a rare occurrence today. Many people will take a "none of my business" approach.

When my dad was very young, his father used to let him hold the reins to the family mule and plow while they were in the field planting crops. My grandfather would mouth the words that to my dad looked like "double due-eee" to get the mule to move.

Wingate would double over in laughter watching young Paris's expressions mimicking what he thought his dad was saying in trying to get this animal to move. In telling me this story Dad would say, probably with the same expression he had back then with is face all distorted, "mule stupid" and his favorite adult phrase "son-of-a-bitch" but without the "a." I presume Dad's pronunciation would have fallen on the mule's "deaf" ears.

As Clara used more of the tough love approach, Wingate was, in contrast, the more indulgent parent with a jovial laugh for everything. In fact, he too, was at times scolded by Clara if he did something not to her liking. I guess he didn't pay her admonishing any mind as she was his beloved Clara.

Separation

BY THE TIME DAD WAS EIGHT AND A HALF YEARS OLD IN 1923, my grandparents knew they had to do something about his education. They knew they could not send him to a regular public school. In the early 20th century, deafness was still highly misunderstood. Public schools did not have the resources to deal with those kinds of issues and, well, my grandparents just didn't know any school for deaf children even existed. Even if they did, the odds that they would take a Native American whose family had assimilated into Black culture were slim to none. During that time, schools for the Deaf were just as segregated as regular public schools. My father, however, was deaf, not stupid. He saw his siblings going off every morning while he had to hang around the house with his mother.

Every morning he noticed that his sisters got up early, got washed and dressed in their pretty clothes, and left for long periods of the day, then returned home in the afternoon. After watching this routine for some time, he decided that he needed to investigate this curious behavior further. He decided to follow them without their or my grandmother's knowledge. So, one morning he awakened, washed, and dressed himself and then slipped out of the house and followed Elizabeth and Jessie.

The young Paris made sure to stay a bit behind the two girls and, at one point, hid in a ditch so as not to be discovered. They walked for a while until they came to Slaughter Street where Dover's Black school was located. The girls went into the school building, but my dad still had no idea where they were going. After they went in, he ran quickly, opened the door, and slipped inside.

There he found a room with several children seated in rows at tables with books in front of them. The teacher stood at the front of the room, but to Daddy she was just another person in the room. He had no idea what she was doing there except that she was an adult. He could not understand what she was saying so he decided to get a closer look.

He went in and sat at the back of the room. He observed that when the lady moved her mouth some of the children raised their hands. After watching this happen several times, he decided to raise his hand when the other children did.

When the lady spoke and the children all raised their hands, he noticed that they all had also turned around to look at him. He, with his hand raised, had no idea what to do. The teacher, I imagine, had no idea why he was there. It's unlikely she didn't know who he was, and she probably also knew he was deaf. I'm sure there were a few giggles, but the class went on as usual. Daddy was allowed to stay until it was time to go home. He walked back with his sisters, and after having his curiosity quenched, was content to remain at home thereafter.

The whipping he received from his mother when he got home also helped him reach that conclusion.

Jessie was only able to complete her education up to the fourth grade, before she had to withdraw due to her deafness from the mastoid infection. Since she lost her hearing at about the age of nine, her speech was pretty intelligible. During those days, parents felt that the education of sons took precedence over the education of daughters, so Jessie's formal schooling ended.

That didn't change the fact that my grandparents knew they were going to have to do something about educating their oldest son. My father had rudimentary communication skills. He could not communicate effectively with people outside of the home.

The state of Delaware did not open a school for the deaf until The Margaret S. Sterck School for the Deaf in Newark, Delaware, opened for student enrollment in 1969. By then, Daddy was fifty-four years old.

Sometime during 1923, when Daddy was about 8 years of age, a White woman of some importance that probably knew my grandmother from her job working as a cleaning lady in the state government buildings, told my grandmother about a "special school" in Philadelphia that educated deaf children.

"Clara, you know you need to put Paris in a school so he can be educated," she would say.

My grandparents decided that they would follow up on her suggestion. They would take a trip to the Pennsylvania School for the Deaf (PSD) in Germantown, Pennsylvania. PSD was founded in 1820 and was then called the Pennsylvania Institution for the Deaf and Dumb. By the time my father arrived there on November 15, 1923, it had moved three times and was located in the Mt. Airy section of Philadelphia. PSD is the third oldest school in the United States established for Deaf students following The American School in Hartford, Connecticut, and the New York School (Fanwood), originally located in New York City. By 1920, PSD was considered the largest and had the most influence of the established schools for the deaf.

These were boarding schools where children entered at about five or six years of age and spent most of the year except for Christmas, and summer vacation. Children today stay at schools for the Deaf during the weekdays and come home on weekends.

My father, at almost nine years of age, was about to embark on his first formal learning experience. The problem my grandparents had at that point was that PSD did not accept Black students. The school assumed my father was a mulatto and in their presumption, refused to allow him entrance. Schools for the Deaf mirrored the social mores of the time and segregation was the policy of the day.

The Harlem Renaissance was in full swing, literally and figuratively. Louis Armstrong and Duke Ellington were making their first recording. African American artists were making history as choreographers, dancers, painters, musicians, and writers. But an almost nine-year-old boy still couldn't get into the only school in the nearby region that had the ability to educate him.

There were schools for Black deaf children in the state of Maryland and in the South, but since the woman who informed my grandmother told her only about PSD, I have to assume my grandparents were not aware of these other schools, they were too far away, or maybe my grandmother just didn't want her son in a Black segregated school. It's hard to know.

My Aunt Grace remembers that my grandmother had to fiercely talk her way into PSD on my father's behalf. My grandmother finally had to pull forth her Nanticoke Native heritage, negating the school's insistence that dad was Black, and was able to get him into PSD. To my knowledge, he was their first student of color.

Now Daddy would have to live away from home and everything that was familiar to him. He was beyond the traditional age and had no previous schooling or formal language.

When he relayed the story to me of how he began his first day at the school, I cried. Not because of any inherent problem with the school, but because he had no way of knowing why he was there, what to expect, or what was expected of him. My grandparents had no way of telling him about his new school, how he would be learning new things and have new living arrangements. Even though my grandparents used lipreading and had their special gestures they used with their son, those methods could not convey the complexity of what was happening at a level he could understand.

My grandparents packed my father's things and took their son on a Trailways bus to Philadelphia.

"Come on Paris, we need to get a move on," my grandmother said as she gestured to her deaf son who could not hear any of her words.

He had never been on a bus before and had never been anywhere without his siblings. At first, my father thought he was taking a vacation with his parents, but when he noticed that all of the suitcases lined up in the hallway belonged only to him, he got a sinking feeling. He thought that his parents were getting rid of him because of his condition.

As an adult, he would sign the story to me: "Thought mother, father love me no more, send me away. Why? Deaf me, bad boy, me." (My father's responses are in the syntax of ASL. It is more closely aligned with the sentence structures of French and quite different from English syntax.)

I could see the tears well up in his eyes as he told me about this experience. All I could do was just stand there and hug him as he hugged me back.

Stories of deaf children being dropped off at residential schools during this period in history are heartbreaking and plentiful. Most of the children had no language, but there's no way to explain what seems like a heartless act even to a child with language. There was no other way to do it. My father stood at the edge of the school grounds watching my grandparents walk away as they waved goodbye, leaving him in a place he'd never been, feeling alone and confused with people he didn't know, for reasons he didn't understand. I'm sure it was just as difficult for my grandparents to have to leave their son behind in that manner.

As a parent, I cannot imagine the loneliness my father felt that first day. He had been surrounded by family his entire life, and now his parents were entrusting him to the care of strangers. But my grandparents knew that my father needed this, so they steeled themselves against the natural desire to coddle him and trusted their instincts. It is amazing the strength parents find within themselves to do what is best for their child even when it tears their hearts apart to see them suffer.

After my grandparents' departure, Dad was taken to his room by a school authority figure. A little while later, Dad noticed a White boy standing outside the dorm room door. The boy appeared to be afraid to come into the room; he just stood there watching Dad put his things away. This boy turned out to be Dad's roommate, and like most students, he had not had much contact with anyone of color. The boy was probably as confused as Daddy. But they were children, and children seem to make sense of their world much faster than adults.

It took my father a few weeks, maybe months, to find his bearings, figure out what he was doing there and what his parents wanted him to accomplish while he was there. He felt a bit self-conscious in the classroom because he was the oldest and tallest kid in his class of six-year-olds.

As with any child, once you send them to school, they no longer totally belong to you. They belong to the world then, and the world teaches them all sorts of things. Some of the things you are glad they learn, even when they come at the expense of your child's happiness.

There are other things we'd rather our children never learn. Daddy was no different. Daddy mentioned that several of the kids would call him "nigger" to which he would reply, "No, Indian, Nanticoke me!" Since Daddy didn't talk about other racial incidents, I assumed after a while he and the majority of students got along.

One of the bad habits Daddy picked up while at school was during meal times. The first few days of school, Daddy didn't get to eat much. This was because there was already an established routine where the boys would eye a particular piece of meat they thought was a choice morsel. During grace, each boy would lick his finger and quickly touch it to the piece of meat he had been watching so that no one else would take it.

Daddy, being a newbie, didn't understand this practice and often didn't get to "mark" any meat before it was all gone.

It didn't take long for him to get the hang of things, though. He quickly learned how to stave off hunger and get the piece of meat he wanted by using the same tactics. When he came home for visits, he promptly learned, with a swat of his hands from his mother Clara, that school was school and home was home. And if he wanted to eat at home, he would use proper table manners.

Not everything he learned at PSD was an affront to civilized social skills. It was at PSD that he learned American Sign Language. While signing was not allowed in the classroom, the students signed in the dorms after classes. This was the time when oralism, the focus on speech, training in lipreading, and the amplification of any residual hearing prevailed.

Up until 1880, the residential schools for deaf children used sign language to communicate with and teach the students. In that year, however, a conference of educators and administrators from schools for the deaf met in Milan, Italy, and voted overwhelmingly to reverse this practice. Believing Alexander Graham Bell's misguided notion that the use of sign language was detrimental to the development of speech, almost all of the schools for the deaf were strictly oral until the 1970s.

During classes and school-sanctioned social activities, students learned to improve their speech and lipreading skills. Daddy, like most deaf students, struggled with speech and lipreading, and the constant drills and memorization of how sounds, syllables, and words should be pronounced . . . puh, puh, buh, buh, mmmm, mmmm, nnnn, nnnn. It was all part of every deaf child's school routine, and to Dad's recollection, no one looked forward to it.

Over time, however, he came to love PSD. He played on the football team and broke his pinky finger doing so. He was on the basketball and baseball teams as well. In fact, Daddy caught the first pitch thrown by the governor (or some equally important official) during one of his games.

As the young Paris became old enough to enter the vocational school at PSD, he switched from specializing in carpentry to shoemaking, the skill at which he would one day make a successful living. Daddy initially thought he wanted to be a carpenter because that was one of the skills his father had. His teachers felt, however, that after spending some time in the carpentry department, shoemaking would be a better fit.

My dad, James Paris Mosley, on the left side of the photo and his basketball team at PSD in 1934.

Suddenly a whole new world of understanding was open to him through this new language. When Daddy would return home for those Christmas and summer vacations, he would teach his late-deafened sister Jessie everything he learned. He shared with her his new language of signs, which helped the two of them form an even stronger bond.

Ironically, the schools for Black deaf children in the South and in Maryland used the manual method; however, many of the signs used in these institutions were what we now call Black ASL. They were different from the signs Daddy learned at PSD. Much of the information about these signs evaporated during the migration of Blacks from the South to the North as southern Black Deaf students had to assimilate into the prevailing dominant northern Deaf culture. Fortunately, we have people like Dr. Ernest Hairston, Linwood D. Smith, James Woodward, Dr. Carolyn McCaskill, and Dr. Anthony Aramburo, to thank for their illuminating research on the history of segregated schools for Deaf students and Black signs.

During their adult years, both my parents went to the Black Deaf Clubs in Philly and New York. Perhaps they were able to meet some of the alumni of these southern institutions. I am not sure if my parents ever learned any of the Black signs that were used in the South. However, they did use the regional signs from the Philadelphia and Maryland area. For example, the sign for "slow" that I grew up using is a thumb to the cheek and the other four fingers close together pressed downward. This is different from the sign used in the Cleveland, Ohio, area, which is a five handshape on the dominant hand slowly moving up the hand and arm of the nondominant hand. Perhaps what was regarded as a regional sign could also have been a Black sign.

A few years after Daddy was permitted to enter PSD, another hard of hearing African American boy from Dover who I eventually and respectfully referred to as Mr. Smike, was the next person of color from Dover to gain entrance to PSD. Daddy and Smike Carter, a slightly built man and a tad bit shorter than my dad, became friends and remained so throughout their adult lives.

Hit and Run

WHILE MY FATHER WAS MAKING HIS WAY AT PSD, LIFE went on as usual at home. My grandparents continued to farm and work their day jobs, and my aunts and uncles went on about their lives as well. The stock market crashed and the country entered the Depression, not that that meant much to the family on Railroad Avenue. They would have bigger worries. My father was twenty or so and had been at school for eleven or twelve years when the tragedy struck.

One misty evening back in Dover, Warren, Jessie, and Grace were walking with my grandmother as she headed to the store to buy my cousin Charles new clothes for the start of school. Charles was the first child of Mommom and Uncle Pick, and the first grandson in the Mosley family. My grandmother wanted him dressed right for his first days of school and apparently Mommom wasn't doing it to her mother's satisfaction. Charles's features were a combination of his mother and father with a slight edge given to his dad, especially in his older years.

As they passed by the old icehouse where the Salvation Army building now stands, a car approached them from behind and ran into my grandmother and Jessie. The driver of the car was a dairy farmer from Marydel. He was headed to the Pet Milk facility with his milk for processing. Grace and Warren, who were walking ahead, missed the catastrophe. My grandmother fell on top of Jessie as the car swerved by and hit them. The driver kept going for a bit, but eventually did turn around and come back to help. They got my grandmother up and put her in the front seat of his car to take her to the hospital. Jessie seemed to be alright except for a limp. With my grandmother in the car came a new dilemma. Grace knew she wasn't supposed to get into a car with strangers and even though her mother was in there she was still afraid to do so. Remember, my grandmother was a strict disciplinarian. Grace told Warren that he should get into the car with my grandmother. Once they'd settled that, they took off for Kent General Hospital, leaving Jessie and Grace to run home and tell their father and sister Elizabeth. Another driver, presumably someone they knew, saw them running, picked them up, and drove them home. That driver dropped Jessie and Grace at home, picked up my grandfather, and drove him to the hospital to see about his wife Clara.

In the "colored" section of the hospital, my grandmother suffered even more from the "medical" treatment she was given. The nurses had used a run of the mill scrub brush to remove the remaining debris from her wounds. The pain my grandmother must have suffered is almost unbearable as I am almost certain there was no anesthesia given.

My grandmother seemed to have been recovering from her ordeal, so a few weeks later, Jessie went to the hospital to help dress her mother and bring her home. When she got there, apparently, my grandmother had developed a blood clot and her heart could not pump the blood beyond the clot. Despite the medical care that she received, she never recovered and died shortly after. She was forty-nine years old.

There are no recollections or stories of my father being at his mother's funeral. The fact that he was in Philadelphia at school and that there was no way for them to call him and talk to him because they had no phone suggests that he might not have been told of his mother's passing until he came home for a visit. Remember this was a time before highways that, today, can get you to your destination much more quickly. The family is unclear how Daddy got the news. The idea that the family wrote him a letter has not been discounted either. Whatever the case, these were the problems of deafness in the early twentieth century.

Jessie was diagnosed with cancer fairly soon after the car accident with her mother. She should have been checked by a doctor along with my grandmother at the time of the accident, but she wasn't. She began to have problems especially around the time of her menses. Although she suffered greatly, her siblings remember her saying, "One day I'm going to get up out of this bed." Her sister Elizabeth learned to use a needle to give her injections when the pain became unbearable. She eventually died from her illness while she was only in her late 20s. I have always wished that I could have met my Aunt Jessie. She seemed as though she was a positive yet tough woman who could endure much.

I'm sure that my grandfather must have been devastated by the loss of his beloved Clara and his daughter Jessie, and wondered how he would raise the rest of his family.

The answer to this dilemma was Ethel Mosley, whom he later married. Ethel was very short in stature, perhaps less than 5 feet tall and had a plump figure. She walked with a bit of a side-to-side sway as if she had difficulty balancing her weight. Since she already had the same last name as my grandfather, she never had to get used to a different one. No need to change the monogrammed towels. Not unlike many families that have to get used to having a different woman in the house, Daddy and his siblings found it shall we say . . . a challenge. Ethel seemed to be a nice enough person, as she would refer to everyone as "honey," but I think it was just difficult for the siblings to warm up to a woman that was now taking the place of their mother. Ethel was now the woman of the house doing things her way and they just couldn't get used to having a stepmother and doing things differently. They eventually grew up and moved out as soon as they could.

Being a Man

EVENTUALLY MONTHS TURNED INTO YEARS AND MY DAD graduated from PSD with a diploma and an understanding of carpentry along with a trade of shoemaking. According to his school records, he graduated from PSD in 1938, at the age of twenty-three. It was not unusual for Deaf students to take longer to graduate than hearing students, especially, as in my father's case, if they started school later than other children.

Daddy landed his first job as a shoe repairman with Tony D'Army on North Governors Avenue in Dover. He worked with Tony for many years and enjoyed honing his skills, but Daddy wanted something else. Daddy wanted to own his own shoe repair business. His father encouraged him to follow his dreams and gave Daddy a parcel of land adjacent to the family home to do just that. Daddy was able to build a small shop that would become known as Mosley's Shoe Hospital, the business that would support us until I was nearly ten years old.

Shoe repair shops require a lot of complicated and expensive machinery. In today's market, a used McKay Stitching Machine could run about $9,000 or more, and that is one of the smaller pieces of equipment. A finisher with all of its brushes, sanding, and trimming units would cost much more. But Daddy was a saver. He was able to save enough from working all those years with Tony to purchase used equipment to start his own business. Daddy cultivated a strong clientele at Mosley's Shoe Hospital and became known as one of the best shoe repairmen around.

Once he got his business up and running, he decided it was time to settle down. Daddy was not necessarily short on prospects. He was a good looking man with his own business, and he was Deaf. Communication is important in any relationship, whether casual or serious. Daddy's problem was that there weren't any women in Dover who could engage in simple communication with him. He couldn't leave his business and go elsewhere in search of a wife, so he opted for the suggestions of friends and family.

Enter my mother.

My mother had attended and graduated from the Western Pennsylvania School for the Deaf (WPSD). Her parents had tried to enroll her in the Pennsylvania School for the Deaf in Philadelphia, where my father had attended; however, they were unsuccessful because PSD was still segregated. When I asked my mother's sister Alice why my father was able to go to PSD and not my mother, her response was, "Well, yo Daddy was yella."

My mother remembers there being only four or five other Black girls at WPSD when she arrived and how overwhelmed she felt in the presence of so many White people. She had grown up in an all-Black neighborhood. She was about 7 or 8 years old and, like my father, did not understand why she was being left at this place. She too had communicated with her parents using gestures. She cried incessantly and held onto her mother's arm pleading not to be left in this strange place. Her parents tried as best they could to make their daughter understand that this was school and that she would learn many things. My mother eventually learned, too, that her parents did what they did out of love.

Her years at WPSD were socially challenging. She did not get along with the few other Black girls that were there and, as a result, found herself on the business end of a lot of physical aggression. When I asked her why she thought she had such a tumultuous relationship with those girls, she replied, "They, maybe, jealous. I attractive, have good communication skills."

Her sister recalls an incident where one of the other girls had cut my mother's hair while she slept. My mother had a long, silky mane of black hair that was often a source of envy. Her parents had to go to the school many times to try and unravel the details of such occurrences. I asked my mother—who is at the time of this writing ninety years young—about this story, but she had no recollection of it.

Having fought her way through WPSD, my mother now tells me of a different story. One of how a girlfriend told her about a Deaf man that lived in Dover that she thought my mother might like to meet. She went on to describe him as being good looking, light skinned, having pretty hair, and owning his own shoe repair business. My mother was agreeable to this set up and went with her friend to Daddy's shoe repair shop.

When they arrived, she asked him if he had a girlfriend, to which he replied, "Yes, but, girlfriend New York live there."

He then asked if she had a boyfriend to which she replied, "No."

My dad asked her if she wanted to go to the movies or something so that they could get to know each other better to which she replied, "Girlfriend have you already. Don't want go out with somebody girlfriend have already." Somehow, she ended up going to the movies with him anyway.

Even as they dated, she did not feel a love connection and certainly had no desire to marry him. The thirteen-year age difference between them did not help matters. But, mothers and fathers want their daughters and sons to live a good, traditional life.

After graduating from WPSD, her parents were concerned about what would come next for their daughter. They wanted her to get married and my dad's parents wanted him to get married. They all supported this union and hoped it would turn out happily ever after. Dad and his father had even built a house for the couple to live in.

When I went back home to visit after having sold the property many years later, the new owner said he wanted to show me something. When he was doing some repairs to the house, he noticed that my dad and grandfather had used old leather shoe soles for insulation between the door frame and the rest of the house. They had to be creative in finding ways to save on costs. Looking at those soles took me back to times of laughter, struggle, frustration, and love. I realized all the hard work my dad must have put in just to provide my mother (and eventually me) a safe and loving home. Despite the media's attention oftentimes on those men who leave their daughters fatherless, my dad was the exception.

So, in 1949, there was a wedding. Only a few family members and friends attended. My mother's marriage to Dad was the result of parents, his and hers, and others who thought the dramatic commonality of their deafness would be enough to sustain a lifelong commitment. It's a fairly benign assumption. Maybe they even thought that Mom's association with Dad would be a calming influence in her life. She was young and was— and still is—quite beautiful. Even today, at ninety, she looks much younger than she really is. Men loved her looks. And she loved to enjoy life.

Dad, on the other hand, was well into his thirties with a thriving business. He wanted to settle down and raise a family. Mom had different ideas. She wanted to enjoy life in that delicious manner of one's early twenties. She was finally old enough to do most of what she wanted and still young enough to get away with it.

My mother recalls that not only did she not want to marry my father, she didn't even want to kiss him when the minister said, "You may now kiss your bride." My mother shook her head no and looked over at her mother Agnes. Her mother, who was now frantically pointing to her own lips, then to her daughter, and then to my dad, was trying to get her daughter to cooperate. My mother resisted as long as she could. Finally, there was a kiss. I cannot imagine my father's feelings at that moment knowing that my mother didn't even want to kiss him.

While the rumblings of Civil Rights began to stir the country into a boiling pot of anger, resentment, and violence, life in Dover went on pretty much as it always had for my father and mother. They had their own boiling pots to worry about.

I am unsure what their marriage was like before I was born. I'm sure they must have had their good moments. However, considering that my mother didn't even want to kiss my father at their wedding let alone marry him, I suspect that things got pretty bad long before I arrived. I know from family pictures that they would go to the Black Deaf Clubs in either Philadelphia or New York and mingle with their Deaf friends. These social clubs were forerunners of today's more political Black Deaf Advocates organizations. During the days of segregation, Black Deaf people had to create their own social outlets as they were not permitted to attend the White Deaf clubs and events. Going to these clubs helped to break up the repetitive social life or lack thereof with the only other four Deaf and hard of hearing friends they had in small town Dover.

Daddy shared how they would play music at the Black Deaf Clubs because even though they were Deaf it didn't mean that they could not appreciate some of its aspects. They could pick up a beat coming through the vibrations of a wooden floor, or read the large signs that hung overhead stating that the music was a Waltz or a Fox Trot.

When the additional pressures of folks asking when they were going to have children began, my mother really did not want to have a baby. I can understand how the idea of a child (even me) might not bring her the

Left of center: Dad and Mom with their friends at a Black Deaf Club.

joy it brought a more willing participant. When she found out that she had conceived, it took her a while to resign herself to the idea of bearing a child. Once she did, she decided she wanted a boy. So, once again, she was not happy when, on March 28, 1953, they told her I was a girl.

Why my mother didn't want a girl I don't know. Even now she offers me no explanation for her desire to have boys. I can guess though that having been forced into a loveless marriage (at least on her part) could make a girl wish for the freedom of men. My mother, I'm sure, saw herself as stuck, and a child was only digging the stakes in deeper. Also, it was part of the times in which she lived. It seems as though my mother was a shining example of what Hanna Rosin so eloquently stated in "The End of Men," an article in the *Atlantic* (July/August 2010).

> For nearly as long as civilization has existed, patriarchy—enforced through the rights of the firstborn son—has been the organizing principle, with few exceptions. Men in ancient Greece tied off their left testicle in an effort to produce male heirs; women have killed themselves (or been killed) for failing to bear sons. In her iconic 1949 book, *The Second Sex,* the French feminist Simone de Beauvoir suggested that women so detested their own "feminine condition" that they regarded their newborn daughters with irritation and disgust.

I do not have many memories of my mother as my parents separated the first time when I was three and then again when I was four years old. I can recall, however, sitting at the kitchen table between the two of them, each one at the table's end. We were eating fish. I remember the conversation between them in American Sign Language that discussed my adeptness with removing the bones.

"Baby smart, know how fish bones take out," Daddy said.

Mother replied, "Yes, baby smart," with a rub of my back.

They of course had removed the major ones, but there was always that chance of a small bone getting by them. I would diligently roll the small piece of flesh around in my mouth until there was no way any piece of bone could have escaped my labor. They seemed so amazed with my skill!

Why I should remember that, I don't know. It is the only memory of her I have when my parents lived together. I know from what my dad told me that I could sign and understand my parent's signs before I could talk. Since motor skills develop faster than vocal ability babies are able to sign before they can speak. That is why so many parents today who can hear teach their babies who can also hear what is known as "baby signs." These are the initial signs for words important to toddlers such as "more," "milk," "cookie," etc.

Communicating using these signs before a child can vocalize, gives them the ability to communicate their wants and needs at an earlier age, thus reducing frustration. At the same time, I was exposed to speech from the very beginning because my parents plus a few of their friends were the only Deaf people in Dover's small community. The saying "It takes a village to raise a child" held true for me because living in an all-Black neighborhood where everyone was either family or friend with my teachers, doctor, dentist, cousins, Mommom, and Uncle Pick along with TV and radio, all helped me to grow up hearing speech.

As a teen, my dad always made sure I had access to sound. Unlike some of my friends, I had a TV and a sound system that played the radio, records, and 45s in my bedroom. I never had any problems speaking normally, like some Codas have expressed. Because everyone around me except for my parents and their few friends could hear, I realized from around the age of three or four that it was my parents who were different and that everyone else in the world used words to speak. That memory was of a difference and not a deficit. It was like, "oh, your parents have brown hair" versus "mine have black hair."

I, as an adult, can now understand how there were difficulties for both my parents. My father was much older and more concerned with the issues of everyday life. My mother felt trapped, cut off before she could enjoy her youth. She was not fully prepared for all that she faced in this marriage. For her, it was too much.

She's Gone

BY 1957, THE CIVIL RIGHTS MOVEMENT WAS PICKING UP speed, the Emmett Till case had both fascinated and ravaged Black America, and Dr. King was bringing a sense of hope and purpose to a movement that would eventually shake the nation so hard it would never be the same again. Elvis Presley was "All Shook Up," Berry Gordy wrote "Reet Petite," one of his first hits, and Jackie Wilson sang it, and I was four years old when Mom left us for the second time.

It would seem that I wouldn't be old enough to carry such a memory, but I remember her leaving. I don't remember it like people think a child should remember something like that. I'm not filled with bitter resentment nor did I feel particularly abandoned.

"Do you resent her for it?"

They always ask that question, even when they pretend to be too polite to ask. It's etched in the expression they try to suppress but can't, something between pity and wonder. It comes like thunder after a streak of lightning. Sharing that memory with some people can be tricky because convincing them that my world is not dark or bitter or full of self-destruction for want of the woman who gave birth to me is exhausting. But I do remember.

I have forgiven Mom for leaving us the way she did, although I don't remember ever really resenting her for it in the way that would answer that curious question. We talk sometimes now, but the sacred bond between mother and daughter was compromised. So, we have settled on a quiet, occasional acquaintance that seems to grow now each time we connect.

The social and family pressures in 1949 created a marriage that was in all likelihood doomed from the start. In particular, it was at a time when deafness was so grossly misunderstood and segregation not only of the races but also from the hearing population had created limited access to socializing opportunities for Deaf children.

I'm sure my mother's family believed that it was going to be difficult to marry off their Deaf daughter, beautiful though she was. They probably believed that Dad was the only person in the city who understood what it was like to be her. That is not to say they should be blamed, or that in their hearts they did anything wrong. They were looking to make sure their daughter was taken care of. Who could blame them? And in the '40s, marriage was still the standard of female acceptance and worthiness.

Still, the problem remained that Mom liked and wanted more from life and Dad was looking for stability. Even after she left, Dad said very little about Mom, good or bad. Maybe he knew from the start that he had taken on a task bigger than himself. I think he probably did. Maybe he thought he could get her to love him. Maybe he didn't think anything except that he had found a beautiful woman who knew what it was like to be Deaf in a hearing world. Maybe, like the others, that was all he thought they needed.

When Mom left us for good it was nighttime. She hadn't been home since the night before, and Daddy and I were going about our regular routine. When she finally returned home the next day, Dad and she had an argument. I guess maybe Dad had made his peace with things the way they were. We had eaten our dinner, the dishes were put away and things were winding down for the evening. I was too young to tell time so all I know was that it was dark, the kind of dark that is wide and engulfing; the kind of night that makes people feel alone in the world even when they're surrounded by people. The sky was a black tent that someone had punched tiny holes in to let in pins of light.

My father had built our house in such a way that our back door looked out onto my grandparents' driveway. I remember headlights breaking the night like the large glowing eyes of an animal lying in wait. My grandparents' home stood in the shadows behind the beaming headlights of the car.

I was standing next to Daddy while mother went into their bedroom. At four, it's difficult to identify the taste and feel of the air. It's simply a taste and feel, good or bad. I knew that the air was different. Later I would identify that taste and feel as the prickly, salty sensation of change.

When I think back on my beautiful mother coming out of the bedroom with her suitcase, I can't imagine what she must have felt. Having daughters of my own now, I can't possibly imagine the level of disappointment and frustration that would allow a woman to walk out on her child.

Did she love me? Would I ever see her again? Was she just a selfish human being? These are not questions I asked myself until much later in my life at the same time the answers became irrelevant.

I imagine that the release of obligation must have been in the sway of her hips as she ambled toward the headlights that waited for her outside. Was she sassy about it? Did her sauciness mock my father to his face that she was leaving and he was staying? Was her cavalier attitude a ruse to cover the pain she was feeling at leaving us behind? Did she laugh when she got into the car with whoever took her away from us? Were we an anecdote she told to the people she met afterward? Where did she go?

I remember watching my father for signs. I was waiting to know how to feel, how to react to this moment when my mother and his wife was leaving us both. He simply stood there and watched her. So I did too.

All I saw was my mother take herself and her suitcase and head for the door. We followed her to the door, not out of any sense of expectation that we could convince her to stay. Even at four, I seemed to understand that this was not something we could stop. We followed her I think out of a sense of curiosity. At four, it is difficult to imagine a world bigger than the one you currently inhabit. My world was Mom, Dad, me, and a few other important people and places. That my mother was reaching beyond those boundaries was incomprehensible to my four-year-old mind. I simply wanted to see.

My father's curiosity may have been bigger than mine. Perhaps he wanted to see what it was in the world he could not offer her. What was there in the night that drew her so vehemently to it that she could turn her back on stability and family? This was the backbone of the American way after all. Still, he did not beg or plead or argue with her to stay or force her to leave any faster than she was already going. We, the two of us, simply stood watching.

Mother went out the door and walked the path the headlights lighted for her and got into the car. She didn't look back. I like to think it was difficult for her to walk out on her child and that's why she didn't look back. Years later I would learn that the man driving the car would maybe be the father of three of the four sons that she would give birth to.

I looked at my father that black night after the headlights had retreated and begun to light another path for my mother and he looked back at me with no expression I can name today. He wasn't smiling, looking relieved or hurt or betrayed. When he looked at me all I saw was Dad.

I realize now that he must have felt something. He had been married to Mom for 8 years. They'd had a child together. They were tumultuous years, but they were their years. They were the years they had planned a life and a family; they were the years he had looked to for his stability. He summed up the destruction of those expectations in two simple signs to me: "Mother gone."

I understood with the benign understanding only a child can muster. He was telling me a fact and I was receiving it. *Mother gone.* It was the beginning of our partnership.

If he had been more emotional I suppose I would have followed suit. But I had him and he hadn't seemed fazed by her leaving and so I suspect I hadn't felt the need to be fazed by it either. Perhaps he was just being strong for me. Yes, mother was gone, but Dad was still here and that was all that seemed to matter.

He closed the door, blocking the retreat of the headlights, bringing my world back into manageable space, and hobbling his own curiosity, and we went back into the house to begin our lives.

PART 2

Life Goes On

WITH MOM GONE, THE TASK OF RAISING ME FELL MOSTLY to my father who embraced the challenge with all the energy he could muster. Dad quickly became everything to me. He is the one who was there at all the relevant moments in my life, both triumphant and tragic. He was there when my mother left, helping me deal with it in my four-year-old way.

To help pay the bills, Daddy rented out his bedroom to roomers, and Daddy and I shared my room. My bed was right under the side window so that I could feel any breeze that came through on those humid Dover nights. Daddy's was on the opposite side of the room next to the back window. In the first year my mother left us, I began to rock incessantly. And then I sang. I know, you're thinking that Daddy was deaf, so who cared whether or not I sang? But he could hear some of the higher pitched frequencies, and I had no idea my high-pitched singing reached his ears.

He would get up out of bed, lean over my bed, and sign, "sing, sing, sing, stop-it. Sleep need." Then he'd go back to bed. That meant very little to me. I kept right on singing. He must have gotten out of bed three or four times a night to tell me to stop, each time his signing becoming a little more urgent. I don't think Daddy got a full night's sleep for at least a year, having to endure my high-pitched vocalizations.

Another parent, at their wits end, might have instituted some kind of punishment like a time out or whatever the punishment du jour was at the time. But Daddy never did. He never lost his temper. The most I got was a stern warning to stop singing.

It might have been a fluke, one of those things kids do, but likely it was a reaction to losing my mother, a way to comfort myself in the wake of her leaving. If I had known how much my father would be there for me the way I know it now, I probably would not have cost him so much sleep.

Looking back it was kind of funny, the look of wearing patience on his face. I didn't recognize it back then, but now I think he must have been ready to pack his pillow and head to the sofa, a less noisy venue. But he never did. Perhaps he understood in ways that he made sure I never had to know how much had been taken from me that night my mother left and let me work it out my own way. He stayed with me and repeated his mantra every night until eventually, I guess, I did stop singing myself to sleep.

There are so many stories of Daddy's nurturing patience it's hard to separate them. One of the most endearing involves pulling teeth. When I hit the age where my baby teeth were ready to come out, there was no trip to the dentist. Dover had one, but he wasn't for things like that. Baby tooth extraction was a personal matter. Having my teeth pulled was never something I looked forward to. My dad did what just about every other parent we knew did when their child's baby teeth were ready to fall out: the door knob method. In hindsight, it seems like a cruel thing to do to a child, but it was the preferred method. Most of the children I knew had had at least one tooth extracted in this most nonsurgical method. It didn't seem to occur to anybody, not even me, that the tooth might fall out on its own or that maybe I could bite into an apple or something else hard. I, of course, was fearful of this method. Most children were fearful of this method. One of the things about being the child of a Deaf parent is that there is no screaming, no outlet. If you do scream, they won't hear it. I could sign my displeasure but releasing my anger in any kind of vocal way was useless, except for my own personal fulfillment.

Daddy would wait until it got dark and then begin the process. I cannot tell you what it was like to stand there with your tooth tied to the door knob waiting for someone to shut it and thereby extract a part of you from yourself. Unless you have experienced it there is no way to explain the sense of utter helplessness that accompanies such a moment. Even today, when I think about those times, the loneliness I felt standing—like being in the middle of nothingness all alone—they come back with a Technicolor clarity. Nobody could help, even if they wanted to; this was a walk I had to take alone.

When he was done tying the knot he would create a ruse. I was still a young child and easily distracted, thank God. He'd find some way to take my attention off of him and what he was about to do. Usually it consisted of him leaving me for a moment, letting me think that we'd postponed the inevitable for a while. Then he would sneak back in the house and shut the door before I had a chance to protest. The tooth would come flying out, dangling from the thread, while I caught up to what had just happened.

I'll say this for Daddy, though; he was very sensitive to my fear. He never expected to me to take it like a grown up or demanded that I just deal with it. I'm not sure if his method was more or less cruel, but it got the job done and I am not at all scarred by the experience. There were other ways that Daddy showed he loved me that didn't involve psyching me into a false sense of security and then committing some necessary trauma.

Christmas was a special time for me. It was extra special the year that I received my first "big girl" bicycle. It was a fine-looking white and mint green three speed. As far as I was concerned, it was the best bicycle in the whole world. I woke up Christmas morning and nothing else mattered but that bicycle. It was how I got it that showed just one of the countless ways my dad expressed his love for me.

We didn't have a car and the store where Daddy had secretly purchased the bike was quite a few miles away from our home. On Christmas Eve, we had decorated the house and placed our presents to each other under the tree. He told me that I should go to bed early and get more rest since we would be up early in the morning. I did what he asked. While I was asleep, he walked all the way to the store. The store owner had put the previously purchased bike in a safe place for him to pick up after hours. In those days a store owner could do that without fear of theft. That was one of the perks of the small town.

Once Daddy had retrieved the bike, he rode it all the way back home and put it by the tree for me to discover on Christmas morning. God must have wanted me to have that bike because that year on Christmas Day instead of the typical cold and snow, it was an unusual seventy-something degrees outside. I got to ride my bike outside in winter, in a sweater!

Helping Out

AS THE CHILD OF A DEAF PARENT I HAD TO LEARN TO DO all sorts of things for both of us at an early age. Daddy made sacrifices for me and I understood early that there also were things I just had to do. They weren't necessarily sacrifices in that particular sense of the word. I didn't lose anything valuable in the process, not right away. The losses I felt didn't become apparent to me until much later. At five years old, though, I had to know things with a certainty that most children my age didn't really have to be sure about—colors, for instance.

My father's shoe shop was right next to the house and Dad and I beat a steady path between the house and shop every day. I couldn't be far from him because of course he couldn't hear me if something happened, so I spent most of my day tucked away in the shop where he could keep one eye on me and I could keep one eye on him. There was no kindergarten available because school in those days for me and my friends started at first grade. My initial schooling was with Daddy in the shoe shop.

Truly, I loved sitting in the shop with him. There were all kinds of people to watch and of course there was Daddy to watch do his thing. His hands moved with a deliberate precision as he manipulated the leather and worked the machines. He had an intimate relationship with the process of shoe repair, one that came from a true love of what he was doing.

Every now and then Daddy's Deaf friends would come by the shop to either drop off their shoes to be fixed or just to say hello. There was Helen Vincent and the red-haired White guy, Jack. His last name escapes me.

Daddy would continue to work holding a shoe in one hand and occasionally when the other person stopped signing would gesture and sign back, all the while continuing to work. He was very conscientious about keeping the flow of work going. Customers wanted their shoes promptly.

Dad in his shoe shop, Mosley's Shoe
Hospital.

So he made sure they were ready, bagged, ticketed, and on the shelf in a
timely manner.

I didn't know, of course, at the time, how to put this into words but I
knew I loved being with him. Daddy's love of the shop translated to security, warmth, and love to me. I cannot imagine spending my early years
anyplace else. I can still recall the smells of leather and industrial strength
glue. Today, I don't think it would be a good idea to have a child so young
under the constant smell of that glue, but back then we didn't think of
such things. Life in Dover was about practical matters. But I can now use
it as an excuse for any senior moments I may have!

Daddy was a resourceful man. It's one of the things I admire most
about him both then and as I recall memories of him now. It could not
have been easy being a Deaf man in those days, and yet he managed
to maintain his own business with better than moderate success. Daddy
and the customers learned to accommodate the communication gap that
existed between them. Most of the time, they would point or gesture
to the part of the shoe that needed fixing, or mouth simple phrases to
Daddy about what needed to be repaired. It was pretty evident as to what
the problem was. Daddy would nod or use his deaf speech to respond.
Customers were familiar with Daddy and seemed to understand him. If it
were something that was more complex, then I would interpret.

I had my very own table in the shop where I would sit and color and do my ABCs for hours while Daddy worked. When a customer came into the store, I was always momentarily distracted. I would watch as my father "listened" attentively to what the customer said. I also had to pay attention in case my father needed me to interpret. I had to. In a minute I could be called upon to do my part.

Daddy was resourceful, but Daddy was also color blind. Even in a small town like Dover it is possible to keep a few secrets. The customer, knowing Daddy was Deaf, but having no clue about his colorblindness, would point to the shoes and then point to the color palette he kept on the counter. Daddy smiled with confidence and nodded, took the shoes and wrote up the order. The customer, satisfied that Daddy had understood, thanked him, turned to me, smiled and patted me on the head, and left the store.

Daddy turned to me, as I knew he would. I was already putting down my crayon and heading over to the counter. He signed, "color black, blue, which?" and I would tell him the color of the shoe and which container had the correct color the customer wanted. I don't know if customers ever caught on to our "shtick" but they kept coming, so we must have been doing something right.

I was also privy to all sorts of things most children my age don't learn until much later in their education. In addition to counting change, listening to the customers talking amongst themselves, and to my father, I learned about the ups and downs of life in general. Because I had to interpret for Daddy, I got to hear conversations for which most children got sent out of the room. Down the line I think that did more harm than good. But at the time, the only way Daddy could participate was if I stayed in the room.

While I was learning the physical aspect of language, Daddy was figuring out how I would manage another side of communication—the telephone, for instance. Obviously Daddy had no use for a telephone. Such devices that exist now for those who are deaf or hard of hearing were either nonexistent or still in their embryonic stages in the 1950s. We had a telephone, but I didn't know how to use it (I was five years old), and with my father and I being alone in the house there was plenty of opportunity for an unchecked emergency to happen.

It so happened that my father enlisted the support of Mr. Stevenson, who I called Uncle Buddy. He was a fifth-grade teacher at Booker T. Washington Elementary School, the elementary school for all the Black kids of Dover. He was a family friend who had grown up with Daddy and all his siblings. Mommom worked for Uncle Buddy's brother, Howard, at his funeral home helping with the preparation and embalming process. She also assisted during wakes and funerals. Uncle Buddy and his wife, Courtney, lived in the first house my grandparents built after living on Railroad Avenue, but lost during the Depression. Daddy arranged for Uncle Buddy and his wife to call our house at 6 p.m. so I could learn to use the phone.

At 6 p.m. sharp the phone rang. Daddy looked at the clock and then at me, and I scurried over to the telephone. I picked up the receiver as I had watched Mommom do, and spoke.

"Hello," I said in my best big girl voice.

"How are you?" Uncle Buddy said.

"I'm fine," I replied.

He then asked, "So, what are you doing right now?"

"I'm helping Daddy cook dinner."

"Okay, we will talk again soon. Have a nice night," he said.

"Goodbye," I answered.

I placed the handset back on the cradle and looked at my father. Had I done it right? Had I learned to use the phone?

Daddy's beam told me all I needed to know. I'm not sure who felt more triumphant that day, him or me.

Without sound, my father understood the value of language, which most of us take for granted. We often see language as a function of sound. We speak and we are heard.

I was blessed because my father knew that I needed sound because sound was a part of my world. As a child who could use spoken language, I would need it to communicate. I would need it to help Daddy. As a child who lived with a Deaf parent, he gave me insight into language I would never have developed in other circumstances.

Who Was That Woman?

I NEVER WENT TO FORMAL KINDERGARTEN. THERE WAS none available to me. Kindergarten was not seen as the necessary component to free public education as it is today. That is not to say I didn't learn anything. Dad took on the responsibility of teaching me what I needed to know. In the shop I learned my colors, shapes, animals, numbers, and my ABCs. Much like today's home-schooled children, I was exposed to experiences that helped me shape my world.

However, apparently not everyone in the community was as sure about Dad's educational plan. We never knew who it was that wasn't sure I was getting a proper education, but one day Daddy and I were both in the kitchen having our lunch when we got an unexpected visitor. Daddy always faced the front door so he could see the doorbell flash. Like other Deaf people, we had a light above the door frame, and when people pushed the doorbell, the light would flash. It wasn't a very bright light, so we had to constantly monitor it to see if anyone was there. If we weren't looking at it, we would never know it was flashing.

When we got to the door, we saw an austere, odd-looking White woman wearing horned-rimmed glasses carrying a thick satchel. My dad nodded to let her in and I did. She marched into our home with the confidence of one who is always right. Daddy and I were not frightened by this woman's appearance in our domain. We were more curious than anything as White people rarely if ever showed up in our neighborhood unless they were bringing shoes to Daddy's shop to be fixed. They never visited our home.

We followed her to the kitchen where she laid her briefcase on the table, opened it, and began to unload all manner of toys. My father watched her patiently. I was thrilled. She had animals of every species and blocks and letters, and I just thought the bounty would never end.

She handed me one item at a time and asked me questions.

"Can you tell me what this is?"

I did it without blinking. "A cow," I said assuredly.

"And what sound does a cow make?"

I produced the guttural reverberation that actually sounded like the utterances cows really make instead of the classic response "moo."

She looked at me quizzically and moved on. "I'm going to show you some numbers. Can you tell me what they are?"

Not only did I tell her, but I signed them to her at the same time. "1, 2, 3, 4. . .10!"

There was no feedback after my stellar performance. She just continued with the next question.

"Can you name these colors for me?"

I responded as I did with the numbers, speaking and signing at the same time, "red, blue, yellow, green, orange . . . purple!"

Daddy knew what I needed to know and he had made sure I knew it. He was an awesome teacher! What he could not help me with, I could get from watching TV, listening to the radio, and talking with relatives and friends.

I guess I passed her tests because without a word, the woman packed up her things and was gone in the same manner in which she had arrived, a little like the Cat in the Hat. We never found out who exactly she was and we never found out what she had to say about what I did or did not know. We suspected that someone who knew I was getting pretty close to being of school age wanted to be sure I was getting educated. Or, maybe someone felt that a Deaf man could not properly teach me what I needed to know to be ready for the world. Whatever happened, things didn't change much after she left. Nobody came and hauled me away, no letters appeared encouraging my dad to send me to some special program. She faded to the back of our minds, becoming another story in our journey.

The Wilsons

I DON'T REMEMBER MOST OF THE COUPLES WHO RENTED the second bedroom in our house. Most of them were associated with Dover Air Force Base, so they came and went pretty frequently, mostly through no choice of their own.

One family, though, entered our lives and left a profound mark on me and Daddy. I'll call them the Wilsons because I was too young to remember their names and anybody who could tell me now is long gone. Still, they were like a watermark on our lives. The memory has faded, but if I hold it up to the light I can still see Mrs. Wilson's round cherubic face smiling at me. Her husband was in the Air Force. They were childless, but that didn't stop Mrs. Wilson from treating me like a daughter. She blew into my life like a fresh, cleansing wind and picked up where other women had failed to make an impression.

Renting our second bedroom also came with use of the house. So the Wilsons did more than just rent out a bedroom. Mrs. Wilson absorbed my daily care like a great sponge. She cooked and cleaned and became our house-mother. Daddy loved having her around because he didn't have to have one eye on his shop and one back at the house on me. I loved it because with her presence came a little more freedom for me. As much as I loved spending time with Daddy in the shoe shop, there were times when I wished I could just stay in the house.

She had a beautiful smile. It was a moon erupting onto a starless night. When I think about that period in my life her smile is the first thing I see. It was one of those smiles that seemed to hold whole universes. It was wide and full of a set of bright whiteness. And it was warm. Some smiles have a way of sending spiders crawling up your spine. I have seen people smile bright smiles that they wanted me to think were warm, but the chill was active and alive and not so far beneath the surface. Hers was genuine. Five-year-olds know.

My most vivid memory involves her washing my hair. I recall that when she washed my hair, the water on my neck felt like tiny pleasant vibrations. Maybe it wasn't the water at all; maybe it was her fingers and the way they felt bracing my neck and head and tickling my scalp. Maybe it was all an extension of that lovely smile. Whatever it was, thinking about it even now makes the back of my neck tingle with the memory of her touch.

At five years old and motherless I didn't need much coaxing to fall in love with a woman who treated me like her very own. My father was and would continue to be both father and mother to me, but Mrs. Wilson, she was my very own nanny.

I benefited daily from her desire to be somebody's mother. She scrubbed me clean and then lotioned me until I shined. She let me help around the house and in return I let her expand into the role of motherhood for which she seemed to have been born. I didn't know why she didn't have any children and frankly, I have to say, I didn't care. I was just glad she was with us and that I didn't have to share her.

I don't need to tell you the heartbreak I felt when they left as suddenly as they'd come. I think my father and I could have handled it better if we'd known why they left. Sometimes children are not privy to the reasons why grown-ups do the things they do. We have to wait patiently until we are grown and circumstances bring us back around to the covert world of adult business that veiled our original curiosity. That was not the case here. Even my dad didn't know why they left. Thus, I was assigned a new kind of interpreting—Dad and I went over to their new "digs" and asked them why they left.

They didn't have a real good answer. They might even have been a little embarrassed at our brazen forthrightness. We didn't care. I know I didn't, and since I took my cues from Dad, I'm pretty sure he didn't either. I wanted those hands in my hair again. I wanted that moon to break through the night just for me. My father wanted a trustworthy pair of eyes back at the house. Our reasons were purely selfish. Renting the room was not a problem. There was always somebody looking for a place to stay. But we wanted *her*.

I remember her saying something like they left for more room (which could not have been the case because the space they moved to was smaller than what they had access to in our home) or some other shielding falsehood. Later during one of our regular chats, Dad and I decided that her husband was the impetus for their hasty departure.

Our theory went something like this: Mr. Wilson got a little antsy with his wife cozying up to the young daughter of the single man they rented their living space from. Mr. Wilson was gone all day, Dad worked just across the path and well, you can kind of see where things might get a little sticky.

So Dad and I were on our own once again. We didn't mind. We loved Mrs. Wilson and her help was invaluable to Dad, but Dad and I didn't need anybody except each other. We settled into our life without Mrs. Wilson, each of us adjusting to the space she left in our own way. In time we got over her leaving us and our lives went on as usual.

Preparation for School

UNLIKE DADDY SOME THIRTY YEARS BEFORE, WHEN IT WAS time for me to go to school, I knew what was coming. For the past year, I had been watching my friends from the steps of my front porch as they filed by my house on their way to school. One of my first childhood friends, Sheila McDowell, who lived right across the street from me, had started school already, and I couldn't wait to join her. All the kids would have on their nice school clothes as they gathered in small packs to meander their way through the streets toward Booker T. Washington Elementary School at the end of my street. I wanted to be where they were and do what they were doing. I never contemplated following them like Daddy did with his sisters, but I was more than ready to go when it was my turn.

Generally, girls have their mothers to help them get ready for their very first day of school, teach them the girly things, and give them advice. But for that very first day of school and all the ones thereafter, Daddy and I had our own little ritual.

There was a general store in the city of Wilmington, one hour drive from Dover, called Wilmington Dry Goods. It was a lot like what we know now as a dollar store, but on a larger scale—a department dollar store. It sold all kinds of things, clothing, housewares, hardware, underwear, you name it. We would get on the big red-and-white Trailways bus and head for the big city where we'd spend the entire day roaming and shopping in Wilmington and its dry goods store. Wilmington was much more metropolitan than Dover. It was alive with people and noises and things to see and do. My eyes couldn't get enough. There were so many streets with stores in Wilmington, unlike Dover, which just had one main street shopping area. At lunch, we'd head to the counter at the local Woolworth's five-and-dime store. Dad would treat me to whatever I wanted, which was usually a chicken salad sandwich with lettuce, tomato, and white cheese. It would usually come with a side of freshly made french fries and a soda of your choice, in my case, Coke. Daddy would get the same. When we had our fill and had shopped till we dropped, we'd walk to the bus station to come back home on the Trailways bus with all our packages. I felt like the richest girl in the world. I had no idea back then that we were shopping at a discount store. I'm not sure I would have cared if I'd known. I was just a girl with her Dad, shopping. None of the other kids got to ride on a bus to go to the big city to buy their school clothes. It made going to school even more of an adventure than I had originally imagined.

On the night before the first day of school, I could barely be contained. I had stopped the incessant rocking and singing, but I would not let myself be calmed. I'm sure I tested Daddy's patience, but I'm also sure he knew precisely how I was feeling. We had laid out my clothes that I would wear the night before and my book bag was filled with pencils, erasers, and paper.

Then my first day of school finally arrived. Daddy combed my hair back into a ponytail that was a bit off center. It's probably the reason why my cousin Joyce, Mommom's daughter, came by before school as time went along to help out with my hair. Finally, I was going to get to see what everybody else already seemed to know. I would get to follow the crowd into Booker T. Washington Elementary School and be a part of the action. The school was about a block or so from my house, so I walked, falling in line with the crowd of children wearing their crisp new clothes heading in that direction.

Since the school housed grades one through six, older students assisted. They were given a list of the names of new students, the teachers, and classrooms to which they had been assigned. The teachers all waited in their classrooms for their students to arrive lead by the older student helpers. I was assigned to Mrs. Blanche Hickerson's first-grade classroom. I was fascinated. This was not the world of Daddy's shop. And although nothing will ever take the place of my first learning environment, I can't express how excited I was to be in a real classroom. If Daddy had been able to be there, it would have been perfect.

Instead, I had Wilma Harris, who turned out to be a fine substitution. I don't remember formally meeting Wilma. Play dates had not been invented for kids like us yet. She lived behind Mommom's house, down the road and across a couple of streets from my house. My first official memory of Wilma and me is making mud pies. I was something of a mud pie connoisseur back in those days. In any case, Wilma and I found ourselves in Mrs. Hickerson's first-grade class together and we couldn't have been happier.

Wilma and another girl who I would not meet until second grade, Regan Hicks, were always the top two students in the school, but I was right behind them. Missing the kindergarten experience hadn't slowed me down a bit. I stayed near the top of my class straight through my time at Booker T. Washington and through my high school years. School was not particularly difficult for me. I was good at most things, but not everything. I discovered later that math was not my strong suit. Well, not all math, mainly algebra.

It was in school that I could measure my life as I knew it by the lives of my friends and other kids. School was where you could discover your personality and gifts, as well as your flaws. I found that I was bright, outgoing, loved to be outdoors, adventurous, had personality and charm, and was willing to try anything once. Challenges afforded you the opportunity to learn the age old lesson that failing is okay as long as you get back up and try again.

I remember receiving a poor grade on a third-grade math test that rocked me. I had dealt with adversity and rejection, but this was different. I had to admit that I didn't understand something and had to seek assistance to correct it. Learning experiences like this help you discover that everyone, including you, has strengths and weaknesses and that you are really not that different from anyone else. Sure you bring unique gifts, talents, and skills to your experiences, but it's the challenges that get the extra credit for helping us to grow and become our best selves. As difficult as it may be, these challenges deserve our thanks.

Mud Pies

SHORTLY AFTER WE LOST THE WILSONS AND I STARTED first grade—and lacking any real activity to keep me busy during the weekends—I decided I was going to make mud pies. Of course, to make a proper mud pie you need water, or else what you have is just dirt. So, I did what any free-thinking six-year-old would do. I scoured the house for the most available vessel to haul my water. What I came up with was a Listerine bottle. Now, it's important to remember that this is the 1950s and child safety was not necessarily the concern of those involved in product development. Translation: Listerine bottles were glass. Children were considered the province of their parents at that time and parents were expected to monitor everything their child was doing. As a child of a single, working, Deaf man, Listerine hadn't quite made provisions for a child like me yet.

Here is why Listerine bottles are now made with child-safe plastic.

I found my water vessel in the bathroom and filled the previously almost empty bottle full of water. At this point the water bottle and I nearly weighed about the same. But at six the world is full of possibility. There is very little a six-year-old doesn't think she can do and without the intrusion of adult skepticism, there is very little she won't try. I was quite proud of my genius. I had enough water to create a veritable bakery of mud without having to constantly interrupt my play with the mundane task of refills. And I had done it without bothering anybody, which at six is a pretty neat thing.

I was almost ready to get to the business of my muddy confection. I hoisted the bottle out of the sink and began making my way back to the front yard. I pushed open the front door and stepped outside, and I wish I could tell you what happened next but the memory dims until I reach the bottom of the porch steps and my right wrist is bleeding out all the blood I have in my body.

My first impulse I'm sure was to scream, but remember, my father can't hear those kinds of things, especially with all that was physically between us. I'm sure I screamed anyway, but I also ran into my father's shop. I can only imagine what he must have thought and felt at that moment when his only child for whom he carried sole responsibility stood before him looking for all the world like something out of a B-horror movie. My body was expelling blood in never-ending currents.

My father, who must have been terrified beyond any words, put me in a chair with my arm propped up, ran to our bathroom, and got a towel to make a tourniquet for me. He was able to stop the bleeding long enough to drive me to the doctor's office. Today, the hospital would have been the wiser choice, but my father grew up in the era of segregation and Jim Crow. The way he saw things, he didn't have time for the evilness of prejudice, which might turn him, and more importantly his bleeding daughter, away because the doctor was not with him or because doctor had not notified the hospital ahead of time that we would be coming. He needed results now, not a wild goose chase. Did I mention I had basically cut a hole in my wrist? I could see straight through.

Doctor Dennis told him to take me straight to the hospital and that he would meet us there. Daddy followed the doctor's orders and sped away quickly in our 1940-something automobile. I think it was a Pontiac. At the hospital, they told him I was lucky. Very lucky! I hadn't cut anything serious. It is true, I guess, that God looks out for babies and fools. After being given ether (yes, that's what they used then as anesthesia) to put me under, they cleaned and sutured my wound, put on a cast, wrapped me up, allowed me to awaken, and then sent me on my way all in the same day.

When I look back on that moment I cannot imagine that my father wasn't feeling a stew of emotions. In order to tend to me, Daddy had to close up his shop and sacrifice an entire day of pay. As a child I didn't think about what that meant. As a parent, I still find it difficult to appreciate fully the sacrifice he made that day. I know in my heart that as his child he did what any loving parent would do. But I am not a single parent who is the sole financial support of my family. He never scolded me for any of it. He only expressed his happiness that I was going to be alright.

We had other less dramatic moments in our lives too. Young children can be a challenge unto themselves. As a mother myself I know that sometimes children just being themselves can work the nerves of the most patient adult.

Work and Wait

I LOVED TALKING TO DAD. WE TALKED ABOUT EVERYTHING. He always seemed to be interested in what I wanted to do or say. In public, we had our own secret language. Daddy and I could comment on the world at large without too much interference.

At that time, American Sign Language was not accepted as a legitimate language. The ability of ASL to handle the rich complexity of language was lost on most people. Today, extensive research by Dr. William Stokoe, Dr. Ceil Lucas, Dr. Scott Liddell, Dr. Robert Johnson, and Dr. Ursula Bellugi as well as others, has shown us that ASL is indeed a true language with all the complexities of spoken languages.

Our most memorable talks came from all the waiting we seemed to do.

This memory starts with an oil furnace. We didn't have a basement in our house so the furnace was beneath the floor in the space between our two bedrooms and in front of the bathroom just off the living room. It was covered by an iron grate. If you've never seen one of those old oil furnaces, you have to appreciate that it is entirely possible to set yourself and the entire house on fire if you don't know what you are doing.

On the side of the house was the oil tank, which would get filled by someone much more experienced than my Dad or me. Unfortunately, he only came once a month and the furnace was constantly going out.

Daddy would climb down under the house and light a match to try to relight the pilot. In hindsight, again, we were quite lucky to have lived as long as we did. When Daddy was done with the fires below he would come up and the two of us would stand over the grate of the freshly lighted furnace, our faces bent down over it watching and waiting. I'm not even sure at this late date what we were waiting for. From an outsider's viewpoint we probably looked like something out of a Bugs Bunny and Wile E. Coyote cartoon. We survived the oil furnace, and when it gave out, Daddy bought us a new gas furnace. Since we didn't have a basement, he had to build a small paneled room in the living room to hold it, taking up even more space in our small house.

We did our own laundry too, what some men would have called "women's work." There were women aplenty in my life who could have shown me things, but most of the time, Dad was my teacher. Eventually, when we upgraded to an automatic washer, washing clothes became my task alone. But, before I was old enough to do it on my own, Dad and I did it together. Every weekend Daddy would roll out the old wringer washer and we'd begin the laundry. Wringer washers required a certain amount of skill so you didn't get your fingers caught in the wringer. Daddy was constantly cautioning me against getting my fingers caught. I guess considering my bout with the Listerine bottle he had earned the right to worry about whether my good sense would get in the way of my curiosity.

He'd hook the machine up to the sink and we'd line up the two washing and rinsing tubs in front of each other in front of the sink and get ready. Today I think about my modern appliances and the time and energy they save and I have to shake my head in wonder.

Sometimes I look back in utter amazement at how my father and I lived through some of the things we did. Our modern conveniences make it difficult for me to comprehend the danger we put ourselves in on a daily basis. But I suppose ignorance is bliss or at the very least contentment.

He washed the clothes, dumping them in the washer, swishing them up and down, and checking to be sure they were clean. It was my job to run them through the rinse and to help Dad put them through the wringer. We didn't talk much over this task because our hands were busy washing, rinsing, and wringing and we were both making sure my hands stayed clear of the wringer!

After all the clothes were washed, we'd take them outside and hang them up on the clothesline with clothes pins to dry. Later, when we acquired our first automatic washer, we would run them over to the local laundromat after washing, stuff them in the dryer, and wait. Here was the treat in doing laundry. While the clothes were drying, Daddy and I would sit and talk for hours about whatever was on our mind.

The doctor's waiting room was another opportunity. Dr. Dennis was our friend and family physician, the one Daddy took me to after the

Listerine bottle incident. During this time, there were no appointments. If you needed to see the doctor, you just showed up.

Dr. Dennis, a Black physician of slight build, was the doctor that all the Black folks went to see. Most of the time, his waiting room was full with chairs lined up all around the perimeter. You could expect to spend several hours that took up much of the day or evening before being seen. But when it was your turn, you had Dr. Dennis's full attention.

To make the hours pass more quickly, Daddy would use his smart sense of humor, and I loved it when he got going. He wasn't always terribly politically correct, though. If he spotted someone wearing a particularly funny looking outfit or with a feature that somehow distinguished them from the crowd he would get my attention, which wasn't hard because I was usually looking right at him, and then make some sign or face about whatever he'd seen that would send me into gales of laughter.

The worst part was whenever I'd get the evil eye from someone who thought children should be seen and not heard. Daddy would straighten his face up immediately and look in a different direction so that no one could tell who or what was causing these outbursts. I would be sobered into obedience for about 5 minutes and then begin a fresh gale of giggles because Dad would be at it again. It made waiting rooms fun and, if I was the one going to the doctor, it made things less scary for me.

Once, we had a small infestation of mice. Daddy set traps and we caught most of them, but one just would not allow himself to be caught. He always took the cheese. Daddy found that to be most curious. Curious enough in fact to make him, and therefore me, stay up one night to see just what this mouse was doing. We turned the lights out with the exception of one night light, which gently illuminated the whole of our tiny house. Soft light spread across the floor and walls giving the impression that we only existed as shadows. We waited.

I have to admit it was pretty boring and Dad had to keep shushing me because I wanted to be busy doing something besides sitting there waiting for that old mouse to come out of his hole. At last, the mouse appeared. Finally, some action! We watched him nibble the cheese and eat all around the deadly part of the trap. The mouse never got close enough to get himself into trouble. I was wide-eyed. It was quite a fascinating scene to watch. The mouse seemed completely unaware that he even had an audience.

The next night, I guess Daddy sensed my boredom because when the nightlight splashed light through the house, he began making shadow puppets on the walls. He had put up a theater just for me. Instead of blank yellow walls I now saw swans and elephants and virtually an entire menagerie of animals popped up to keep me company.

I've said that as long as Daddy was there not much scared me. In hindsight, what stayed with me the most was not so much trapping that mouse, but the whole host of shadow puppets he brought right into our kitchen to keep me happy.

To top it off, Daddy eventually did outsmart the mouse. Mighty Mouse finally met his match.

The Divorce

1960 WAS A BANNER YEAR. MOTOWN RECORDS, WHICH provided the music that became the soundtrack for the next twenty years of my life, officially opened its doors on West Grand Boulevard in Detroit. "Shop Around" by the Miracles featuring Bill "Smokey" Robinson was the very first record I owned.

By then, my dad and I had made peace with the fact that my mother was not coming back. I don't think either of us ever really thought she would, but nothing had been done about it; that is to say, my parents had never officially called an end to their marriage. Somewhere, somehow, Daddy developed a very real fear that my mother might try to come back and take custody of me. I'm not sure where he got that notion. As far as I knew, my mother had not expressed any interest in coming back for me.

After my mother and I reacquainted ourselves later, after I had given birth to my own two daughters and they were grown women in their 20s, we had a conversation about her intentions. She confirmed that the idea had crossed her mind, but that she knew Daddy was the best parent for me. He was stable, and had the assistance of his sister Lib. Given her lifestyle at the time, she was in no position to raise me. She had left her oldest son to be raised by her mother and father and the other three sons to be raised by their aunt while she lived a rough life in New York. She eventually left New York in fear of her life, moved to Baltimore, remarried and settled there.

In any case, Dad got nervous that if he didn't settle this thing and settle it quickly it might turn sour for us. I was game because I couldn't think of a worse fate than having to leave my daddy.

Daddy sat me down at our kitchen table and explained that he wanted to finalize the situation between him and Mom. He thought we both needed the closure, although those weren't the exact words he used. He explained that in order to do this we would have to go to court and talk to a judge. I didn't really understand all the intricacies involved in going to court, but I was down for whatever Daddy wanted. So, Daddy made the arrangements, although I don't know how.

It was an interesting experience trying to get a divorce and formal custody of me without my mother present for any of it. I was a kid about seven or eight years of age, and I learned a lot of legalese in a very short period of time. Daddy didn't have anybody else to interpret for him, so all of the court proceedings had to come through me.

The day arrived when we had to testify in court. Daddy and I went down to the Dover courthouse, both of us a bit nervous. As far as I knew neither of us had ever been there. Daddy held my hand as we headed inside the Kent County Courthouse.

Inside, I wished I had been blessed with the ability not to hear our footsteps reverberating against the wooden floors. We couldn't possibly have been the only people in the courthouse that day, but I don't remember anyone or anything else. All I remember is the ominous sound of heels against wood as we made our way to the appointed courtroom.

Our lawyers were White, but sympathetic to the plight of a Deaf man with a young daughter who had to do all of his interpreting. However, they didn't try to make the language very accessible to either of us. They seemed to me to use all the legalese they knew. And they talked fast. I swallowed my frustration and steeled myself for the task at hand, a quality I would come to recognize in myself over and over again as life presented me with obstacles.

I remember being so afraid that if I interpreted something incorrectly or didn't understand how to interpret something, they would take me away from the only parent I knew. He was the only constant in my life. I don't believe I would be the person I am today had I not been able to stay with Daddy. Whatever I did, it must have been okay because when it was done, Daddy had his divorce and custody of me, and nothing ever came of it beyond that moment in court.

We never heard from my mother about it so I guess she was okay with everything. Maybe she didn't even know. At some point she must have known that Daddy had gone ahead with the divorce, but if she had a problem with it, she never said anything to us.

Before and after the divorce, Daddy never dated. There were ladies interested in him, but he ignored their interest and focused on raising me. He stopped traveling to the larger cities to visit his friends too. Occasionally, Mr. Smike would stop by, but Daddy mostly just visited with family and kept his attention on his work and me.

Clink, Clink, Clink:
Interpreting Sounds Not So Silent and Other Things

AS DADDY'S ONLY MEANS OF COMMUNICATING EFFECTIVELY with the wider world, I got to do some pretty tricky signing beyond the courtroom experience. When we can hear we take simple things for granted. For instance, when something is wrong with your car you can usually hear it, like a rattle, a clink, or a squeak. It's nothing for someone to say "my brakes are squeaking" or "my engine's loud," or when it won't start it's easy to say whether there is any sound coming from the ignition at all.

All of those cues are associated with sound, something my father knew next to nothing about. He needed my ears to be his ears and so, whenever we were in the car I would have to listen. A lot of the time I had no idea what I was listening for. I knew very little about cars and how they worked. If I heard something that didn't sound normal, I would have to interpret the sound for Daddy so he would know something was wrong and then we'd have to figure out how to let the mechanic know. I laughed out loud when I read an article in the February 2014 issue of the *AAA Motorist* titled, "You Can Learn A Lot by Listening to Your Car: Signs that Your Vehicle May Be Trying to Tell You Something."

The thing about interpreting sound for someone who is not connected to sound is that it's difficult for them to understand. How do you explain the concept of a "squeak" to someone who has never heard it? What language do you use to help someone understand a concept with which they have little or no experience? That was my dilemma for as long as I can remember. Translating the sounds of the car is just one example of some of the many tasks I spent most of my time working through.

Living in Dover during summer evenings meant listening to the chorus of crickets as they hopped through the grassy areas around our home.

Explaining the noises they made was quite a challenge. Daddy and I would sit on the front porch in our rocking plastic lawn chairs taking in the sights, and for me the sounds, of a major thoroughfare with a heavily frequented liquor store just across the street.

Then there were the times when I was privy to information that probably would have been best kept between grown-ups. Some of the most unique experiences I had were in the doctor's office with my dad. Dad made sacrifices for me throughout his life that I will probably never even know about. And I was glad to do the same for him whenever I could. But those are things I didn't understand until I was much older. What I knew at the time was that I was the only person in my family who could facilitate communication between my father and everyone else.

And for him, it must have been a nightmare. It is bad enough to have to bring your child into the examination room with you. It has to be even worse to have to use her as an interpreter. When the majority of us go into an examination room as adults, our privacy is assumed. My father did not have that luxury. What he had was me.

My father, who must have felt vulnerable, continued to keep his composure during the time the three of us conversed about the very private aspects of his life. Like any adult, my father sometimes had intimate issues that he needed to discuss with the doctor. All of those complaints, both major and minor, had to be interpreted through me. The feeling for me, though, was that it was just another aspect of what I did. Sure, there were times when I wished someone else knew how to sign, but at that time, life was what it was. Looking back, I'm sure he may have felt some embarrassment having to discuss things like frequent urination in front of his child, but we both handled the situation like adults, even though only one of us was.

Daddy was not big on banks. He lived through the Depression, when banks were not the safe havens we consider them today. He worked hard for his money and he was not about to take a chance that one day he'd walk into the bank and find that it had gone belly up with his life savings. He had a bank account, but he didn't put all of his eggs in one basket. Instead, Dad kept his money in the closet on a top shelf in a brown paper bag. He came home one day and found that the bag was not where he thought he'd left it. By the time I came home from school, Daddy was in a state. All he could do was pace and sign over and over, "money gone!"

As I have said before, I took my cues from Dad. If he was worked up, then I was worked up. My heart beat faster, so much so that you could have heard the pounding in my chest, my stomach did flip flops, and my intestines had a real humdinger of a pinball match going.

Much of his entire life's savings had disappeared. We had no idea what could have happened to his money. We searched every room in the house . . . twice. Finally, defeated, we called the police.

When the police arrived they tried to be helpful. They asked Daddy (through an interpretation by me) all the right questions, but Daddy just didn't have the information they needed to be able to move forward with any kind of relevant investigation. He didn't know who could have come in. No, he hadn't told anybody where the money was. The locks had not been tampered with. The doors and windows were all closed and locked.

All the police could do was shrug and promise they'd do the best they could. I closed the door behind them and stared at Daddy. What were we going to do?

Later that night—and this is where the story gets murky—Daddy found his money. He forgot he had moved it. He hadn't told me, so I didn't know.

I wanted to call the police and let them know, but Dad wouldn't let me. I think part of him was profoundly embarrassed. Daddy tucked the money away and the incident was never mentioned again.

Social Changes

I SAW TWO PRESIDENTIAL CANDIDATES DURING MY childhood, John F. Kennedy and Barry Goldwater. Okay, I know what you're thinking now. How in the world does a person get to see Kennedy *and* Goldwater? *Why,* might even be a better question. The answer is simple: that was just Daddy's style. He liked to be informed about who he supported as well as who he didn't support. How else would he have known which was which?

Between the years 1960 and 1968, America underwent massive social changes. The political scene was on fire, the Civil Rights movement was at its peak, Black Power was taking a radical stand, racial violence was breaking out everywhere, students were protesting the war in Vietnam, and women were coming to the end of their collective rope. The advent of television as a useful campaign tool made the Kennedy-Nixon debates in 1960 grist for the mill for years. It was truly a time like no other in our history.

I was a young girl, barely seven years old and in the second grade in 1960. I had a very limited idea of politics and politicians, civil rights, or even women's issues. Vietnam probably wasn't even a word I could pronounce yet. I was still in the backyard making mud pies while history was happening around me. Fortunately, I had Daddy.

Daddy was a Democrat. He read the newspaper religiously, and he kept his finger on the pulse of the American political scene. He seemed to know instinctively when history was in the making and he tried to make sure I was somehow in the middle of it. I learned about what was happening in our society from Daddy. He would have discussions with me at the kitchen table about what he had read. He read his newspaper and would convey his disdain for Nikita Khrushchev. "Khrushchev terrible," he would sign.

When I was older, about age twelve, Daddy made sure I had a television in my bedroom so that I could keep up with late-breaking news stories, which, at the time, seemed to be happening at breakneck speed. It was not only so that I could stay current, but also so that I could keep him informed about what was being talked about on the nightly news.

Even as a candidate, Daddy seemed to have a sense that Kennedy was going to be very important. Maybe the newspaper he stayed draped in gave him insight I, as a child, just could not grasp. Maybe he was just one of those people who had a sense about things. Whatever his reasons, he knew Kennedy was going to be somebody special to minorities.

During his campaign, Kennedy made a stop in Philadelphia. Daddy and I took the Trailways bus to Philly outside Convention Hall so we could see this man about whom all this fuss was being made. It was October 31, 1960. I was seven years old.

The crowd was immense. The courtyard outside Convention Hall seemed huge to me. Even when Daddy hoisted me onto his shoulders so I could see above the crowd, the podium where Kennedy stood seemed light years from us.

At eye level things weren't much better. The area was bursting at the seams with people. Daddy hustled us through the crowd as best he could smiling and nodding, but pushing us through. We still didn't get all that close, but I could see and hear.

Kennedy was as handsome as everybody said he was. He was charismatic, not that I knew what that meant at that age. I did know that the ebb and flow of language kept me riveted. Dad was relying on me to interpret as much of Kennedy's speech for him as I could. Can you imagine? At seven I didn't understand much of what he said, but I tried my best for Daddy and he, as always, seemed satisfied.

When I think about Daddy and the things he knew I needed to know, it amazes me. At that time, he could have sat at home and let me find the world on my own. He could have used my age, his deafness, his age, the racial times, any of those excuses to allow us to sit in the house and absorb all the barriers to our success and nobody would have blamed him. They would have seen the single, Deaf man with a young child and felt pity. But he didn't see things that way.

Daddy lived in this world and he knew what kind of woman he needed to raise to make sure she could live in this world too. Being politically aware was just one aspect of who he wanted me to be.

Daddy and I were both elated when Kennedy won the election over Nixon. During Kennedy's term in office, Daddy continued to read his newspaper and convey his disdain for Nikita Khrushchev. Daddy was concerned, as was the country, of Khrushchev's intentions in the Cuban Missile Crisis. He hoped Kennedy would handle this delicate situation appropriately. "Khrushchev, dangerous! Start war maybe, use missiles there, Cuba, attack US!"

In school, we would have air raid drills that would blast sirens all over the school warning the students to get under their desks or go out to the hallway and get on our knees in front of the lockers, put our heads down, and cover them with our arms and hands. What a scary procedure for elementary school age children!

I don't think that many of the students truly understood why they were engaging in this behavior other than the Russians might attack us and we need to be prepared. I probably had more of an understanding of the details than most kids my age because of Daddy's discussions with me. If the Russians were to really attack us, I'm not sure how much protection a desk or covering our heads in the hallway would have been.

I was ten years old and in school at Booker T. Washington when Kennedy was assassinated in 1963. The announcement came over the public address system. All the students were summarily dismissed to grieve in whatever private way was ours. I knew Daddy didn't know because how could he? It hadn't made the papers yet and he couldn't hear the radio.

I ran home with the news. When I signed the news to Daddy, the look on his face told me precisely how I should feel. His expression revealed that we, a country and a people, had lost someone and something very important. We knew that President Kennedy represented hope for people of color and now that hope was lost. I would see that look on his face when I had to tell him three more times over the course of the next four years that other important men had been shot—Malcolm X in 1965, Dr. Martin Luther King Jr. in April 1968, and Robert Kennedy in June 1968.

In light of that, Daddy also took me to see Barry Goldwater when he came to Dover to campaign in 1964. By then I had to be about ten or eleven years old. Goldwater came directly to Dover. We stood outside in a parking lot and the crowd was not nearly as large as the one for Kennedy. Daddy had no use for Goldwater, but Goldwater was a political candidate and Daddy understood that all the political candidates were important, whether Democrat or Republican. We needed to know what they were all thinking.

What I got from that visit was that Goldwater was everything I thought a typical conservative Republican would be. He looked out at the audience from his horn-rimmed glasses with that condescending expression which is one of the hallmarks of those who think they know what is best for everyone else. It was a look that made me feel like he was saying to me, "I'm not even going to ask you what you need because even if I was willing to listen it wouldn't matter, in the end I'm going to give you what I want you to have, and you're going to like it."

I disliked him instantly. I also knew that Daddy didn't like him. He didn't make it a secret or anything. In the car, he looked at me and sneered "Goldwater" in his Deaf dialect followed by a swat of his hand, suggesting perhaps what he'd like to have someone do to the man.

It wasn't a political moment I remember like I remember seeing Kennedy, but it was important and even though I can recall very little of either man's speech, I recall with pride the fact that I was there. I touched history. I heard it speak. I felt the winds of change blow against my cheeks. And in some small way, imperceptible to me now, I responded.

When these political figures—John and Robert Kennedy, Malcolm X, and Dr. King—were alive and in the prime of their political careers, I, like most if not all Black people in this country, felt a sense of pride and optimism that the future for African Americans and other people of color would be much improved. That finally, as I recited every morning at Booker T. Washington Elementary School, this country would become the ideal of one nation under God with liberty and justice for all. Then, when all these leaders were assassinated one by one, there initially was a feeling of despair and then anger.

But then, I remembered what Daddy taught me: Righteousness always wins. He was not a religious person, never went to church (there were no interpreters). But he was a decent and upright moral man. Sure he had his vices. He enjoyed smoking his cigars and cigarettes. (Until it was discovered these "death sticks" would kill you, then he just quit. Never went back to smoking again.) He loved to have a can of Schlitz, Pabst Blue Ribbon beer, or a Colt 45 Malt Liquor with his evening meal and, on occasion, a shot of Jack Daniels, but he had a moral compass that always pointed toward integrity and virtue.

Yet somehow, in some way, he believed we would overcome. You have to keep on pushin'.

Now Daddy's Leaving Too?!

DADDY AND I LIVED OUR LIVES WITHOUT MUCH WORRY, aside from the occasional incident, until I was about eleven years old. The shoe shop was doing a fair business, renters were still coming and going. Mommom lived fairly close by and acted as the female influence in my life. Things were going well. But of course no path worth walking is ever smooth and straight. Ours was no different.

Our troubles started when the city decided to pave the cinder road on which Daddy's shop and our house sat. Daddy's business suffered because that road was the only road to the shop and while the project was being worked on, no one could get their shoes to Mosley's Shoe Hospital. Daddy had to face the reality that he was going to have to close up his shop and find work somewhere else.

It was not the best time for us. Looking back, I think I understand the trauma now better than I did when I was going through it. I knew it was life changing. My life changed after all. And it changed big. Daddy was the only parent I had, the only person I had learned to count on. And he was leaving me. We had to leave our house. I was to go and live with Mommom and her family for a couple of years or so while Daddy took work in Wilmington. But at the time, I suppose I just thought we were doing what we had to do.

It didn't occur to me consciously until much later that for the second time in my life I was losing a parent. Granted, the circumstances were different. Daddy was coming back. He was not going off to live the life he felt had been deprived him by my presence. But still he was leaving and he wasn't taking me with him.

That's a lot for an eleven-year-old to consider. I didn't know where my mother was, but Daddy was going to Wilmington. He had found work at Walsh Shoe Repair. His sister, my Aunt Jeannette, who lived in

Mommom, Aunt Jeannette, and Aunt Grace.

Wilmington, put him up for the duration of his stay. Our house went up for rent and I went to Queen Street to live with Mommom, Uncle Pick, Uncle Warren, and their daughter Joyce.

By then, their son Charles had already spent time in the Navy, was honorably discharged, and got married to Carrie Mae, his childhood sweetheart. They lived in a small home in Northwest Dover Heights, a neighborhood of African Americans close to the campus of Delaware State College. From that union, Sharon, their only child together, was born. At that time, he was working for the State of Delaware in security.

Staying with Mommom and Uncle Pick was an extension of the life I had experienced before Daddy had to leave. I would often walk the few blocks from my home to theirs after school and stay for dinner. Mommom used to joke with me saying, "How come you always know when we are having steak?"

"I don't know," I would slyly answer back.

"Are you having corn on the cab too?" I would ask.

Everyone would break out into colossal laughter and let me know that it was corn on the cob. She always made an extra space for me at the table. Joyce was about 8 years older than me and was more like a big sister than my first cousin . . . Joyce and I shared a bedroom, played jacks, washed dishes, and cleaned the house together.

During the summer, I would go to Wilmington and stay with Daddy for a few weeks at Aunt Jeannette's house. She lived in an Italian neighborhood. I always looked forward to that time. Aunt Jeannette would fix me "milk tea," which was a cup filled halfway with boiling hot water and then she would pour in PET milk to the brim, add sugar, and yum! Her firstborn was her son Ronnie, then came the sisters Roma and Rita. They would come over from their individual homes as they were young adults (I was the baby of that generation), and we would sit in her long, but narrow backyard with Aunt Jeannette's black-and-white mixed-breed dog running around. We would eat homemade spaghetti with Parmesan cheese (I called it stinky cheese) or crabs that Aunt Jeannette cooked in a huge boiling pot of Old Bay seasoned water.

Those crabs were alive and fierce, but no match for Aunt Jeannette's skill. She would uncover the lid, pick them up from the wooden basket on the floor at the base of the stove one by one, and toss them into that boiling water. After they were cooked, we would put newspaper on tables and spread out the crabs so each person could grab their choice to enjoy. I would break off the legs first and use a small wooden mallet to break open the shell that concealed that sweet white flesh. After the legs had been consumed, I would tackle the center. You had to be careful not to eat the "devil fingers" located at the top of the center part. They were considered toxic and not safe to eat.

It was great to sign with Roma and Daddy because I could be included in their adult conversation. I also enjoyed hanging around Ronnie and Rita because they were about thirteen to fifteen years older than me and seemed so cool to an eleven-year-old. Aunt Jeannette's neighbor, Mr. Guedo, had a kitchen window that was on the side that faced Aunt Jeannette's kitchen window. In the summer, the windows were kept open.

"Hi, Mr. Guedo!" I would holler.

"Hey there. You back again?"

"Yep," I would answer.

But I always had to go back to Dover. It was like traveling between dimensions. I preferred the adult world. By then the world of children did not hold much interest for me.

It's never easy being in someone else's home indefinitely. Not even when your hosts are family. They have their routine and we had ours. Despite the obvious love and affection I got from Mommom, Uncle Pick, Uncle Warren, and my cousin Joyce, I always missed my dad and our familiar routine.

For instance, though my father's family was Nanticoke, we had assimilated into and embraced the Black culture of Dover . . . Daddy watched Black music being danced to by Damita Jo and other regulars on *Soul Train* with me, read the literature of the Black community such as *Sepia*, *Ebony*, *Jet Magazine*, and later, my *Essence* magazines. He generally identified with the Black experience. Daddy and I would have discussions about current events. I could easily gauge where he stood on the issues.

Mommom and Uncle Pick did not have that identity. They did not consciously reject Black culture; instead, they absorbed the farm culture that framed their lives. They listened to the music that spoke to their lives, such as country and whatever else played on Dover's WDOV station. Uncle Pick could often be heard around the house singing, "I'm lookin' over the white hills of Dover" in his country twang.

The developing Motown sound meant little to them beyond having to hear me play on their HiFi the 1964 hits by the Four Tops like "Baby I Need Your Lovin," the Supremes singing "Baby Love," The Temptations singing their 1965 song "Since I Lost My Baby," and all the other popular Motown and Atlantic Records music over and over and over again.

I remember watching on Mommom and Uncle Pick's television the growing unrest that was occurring in the South with the sit-ins at the F. W. Woolworth lunch counter. It was frightening to see how cruel people could be to those young teens, especially when I had such positive memories of Daddy and me going to the F. W. Woolworth in Wilmington for our lunch after shopping for my first days of school clothes at Wilmington Dry Goods.

The news also reported on the freedom riders' confrontations with the Ku Klux Klan, Governor George Wallace's obstruction of Blacks attending Alabama public schools and his impediment to James Hood and Vivian Malone registering at the University of Alabama, police who took an oath to serve and protect unleash vicious dogs and spray heavy water from fire hoses on Black and supportive White teens, and the 1963 March on Washington with the Reverend Dr. Martin Luther King Jr.

Lee Daniels's movie, *The Butler*, documents so well many of these events that I remember watching on TV as they were occurring. The interesting thing about this image is that I don't remember Mommom, Uncle Pick, or anyone else in the house discussing what these events meant to them or to our country. Clearly, it was of interest to them, but there was never an in-depth discussion about what was going on. It was just like watching any other gruesome event on the nightly news that could be happening anywhere. On the other hand, Daddy was engrossed in these historic actions. He seemed to have a need to talk about how horrific it all was.

So, I fit myself into a different plan. I eventually learned to adjust. At this age, I couldn't really put my finger on the sensation that comes with being a semipermanent guest in someone's home. I knew that I was loved. Mommom never made me feel like she didn't want me. But no one in our family was rich. Everybody worked for their living. I was an interloper. I ate what they ate. I used their linens. I washed with their water. Their resources had been allocated for the four people who inhabited their home. Those resources did not, until I moved in, include me. I'm sure Daddy sent her money for my room and board, but I'm also sure it wasn't enough to cover the true cost of my living there. When Uncle Pick gave his daughter Joyce a couple of quarters for her school lunch each day (the cost had gone up by then to fifty cents), he would always give me a couple of quarters too. There were lots of perks to living with Mommom and Uncle Pick. We were a true extended family. Aunt Grace and Uncle Kemp lived next door, until Uncle Kemp was transferred to the Philippines by the Air Force.

We had a dog, a mutt, who we named John Fitzgerald Kennedy III Durham. When he was a puppy, he would never stay in his box that we prepared for him. Joyce and I weren't that close in age, but we were close enough that we could forge a bond of friendship and sisterhood. Mommom had taken in her brother, my Uncle Warren, who was epileptic.

After leaving his parent's home, he always lived with Mommom and Uncle Pick. Because of his seizures he was constantly looked after. This was before the proper medication of today, where people with epilepsy can lead much more independent lives.

Joyce and I often saw Mommom as a source of entertainment. When we lived on Queen Street, once she pulled her coat off the hook she usually hung behind the basement door and tried to put it on. Her arm did an involuntary twitch and for a split second she looked confused. And then sheer terror. And then the shrieking began. When she was able to talk again we discovered that a mouse had used her coat sleeve as a hiding place. None of us would have dared laugh at Mommom to her face, and really I don't think any of us thought it was that funny at the time. But afterward and even now the moment is pure comedy.

Joyce and I loved to sing and sometimes we would harmonize our singing on the song "Going to the Chapel of Love" by The Dixie Cups. Sometimes we would harmonize with our next door neighbor, Mrs. Charmaine Grice. She, like Joyce and I, loved to sing gospel songs. The Queen Street house was a duplex with paper thin walls. Whenever Joyce and I were in the kitchen doing the dishes, we would sing. If Mrs. Charmaine was in her kitchen too, she would hear us, and join in. We had some pretty good harmony coming out of that kitchen.

Playing games of jacks and pick-up sticks was a favorite pastime for Joyce and me. We would sit opposite each other on the dining room linoleum floor that connected the kitchen to the living room. It was right in the middle of the walkway so when we were playing if anyone was trying to pass through, they'd have to delicately step over our legs and then go around.

And there was the Dry Cleaners Truck Man, the Milk Man, the Bread Man, and the Huckster Man. All of these characters delivered their items to your door clean and fresh several days a week depending on your need. It was the Huckster Man, however, that made my neighborhood quite colorful. On many a Saturday we could count on the Huckster Man gracing our street with his presence. He was much like the ice-cream man rolling through the neighborhood playing those annoying tunes as he drove by.

The Huckster Man would come with his truck full of bright crisp vegetables and fruits, screaming his wares. "Huckster Man! Huckster Man here! Get your nice fresh vegetables! We got fresh tomatoes, corn, peas, *wintercrease* greens (winter cress) from the Huckster Man!"

We'd run out to the pickup truck with our money, select from the myriad of freshness on the cart and haul our bounty back into the house ready for Mommom to turn it into something edible and delicious.

Mommom and Uncle Pick also had a huge garden in the back of their home on Queen Street. It was like our very own small farm. We grew corn, cucumbers, tomatoes, string beans, and other vegetables. Whatever we did not grow, we could pick up from the Huckster Man. There was no big machinery to help them plow and harvest their crops. It was just us. I enjoyed spending time with Uncle Pick and learning a new skill. I would help him plant and when it was time, I'd help with the harvest. We'd walk through the rows of soil he would till and then make indentations. For planting corn, it was my job to place three seeds in each hole and cover. After everything was planted, we would water and watch all the vegetables grow. This was not the stuff you learned in a textbook, but it was the learning of life.

Uncle Pick would also go deer and rabbit hunting with his neighborhood buddies. When he brought home rabbits, I got to help him prepare them for the next night's dinner. I would hold the hind legs with the belly up and Uncle Pick held the front legs. I learned at an early age how to cut, clean out, and strip the rabbit of its fur and dunk it in salt water to remove any of the blood and impurities. We would then par boil it in celery and onions that would give it added flavor. Just before we were ready to eat it for dinner, we would coat it in flour and pan fry it in vegetable oil. Now, as an adult, I just enjoy the cute little bunnies and deer that like to run around and play in my backyard while I watch out my kitchen window.

The Huckster man, the garden, and the preparation of venison and fresh rabbit all gave me a strong sense of where my food came from. Today we go to the grocery store, the butcher, the farmers market, and most may not think about where food actually comes from or who grows it, kills it, and prepares it for sale. It's just food we buy.

But I was lucky to have had a sense of all that. Its value to me is limitless. Knowing where your food comes from enhances your sense of being alive and staying alive. Somehow it shines a light on the fact that if you don't work, you don't eat. It's a lesson every child should know.

The best thing about living at Mommom's, though, was that she lived right on the Trailways bus line. Even though Daddy was in Wilmington, he came home to see me every 2 weeks like clockwork, and the bus line was like an asphalt thread connecting our lives.

I would sit on the front porch in one of Mommom's wooden rocking chairs and wait for the bus to pull into town. I was anxious for him to be there not only because I missed him so much, but because it felt like a part of my old life was given back to me when he was home.

Daddy would always try to sit on the left side of the bus so that he would be where I could see him as the bus headed toward its stop further up the street. I would sit patiently until I saw the bus and then my heart would race and I could feel myself becoming whole again.

When the bus would go by, I would wave excitedly, if Daddy was where I could see him. I wanted to make sure he saw me, knew that I was waiting for him. And his waving back said the same thing to me.

Sometime during that period, Mommom and Uncle Pick moved away from Queen Street and built a house in Lincoln Park, a newer development in the African American community near where Daddy and my house was on Forest Street. They had been renting the house on Queen Street for quite a while and felt they should take the opportunity to pursue the American dream of owning their own home. Prior to moving in, we made many trips to the new house to watch the progression of it being built. We got to pick the colors of all the rooms and make decisions about what should go where. The location was great because we moved right next door to Leslie Dewberry and her family.

Leslie and I became great friends. Our houses were exactly the same in architecture except they mirrored each other. Leslie's bedroom window and Joyce's and my shared bedroom window faced each other. Instead of calling each other on the phone, we would just open our windows. The houses were close enough that if we stuck our hands out the window and leaned out we could touch. We'd stick our heads out and talk to each other. We had some great conversations over the air.

We had a lot of fun at Mommom's when she wasn't finding things for Joyce and me to clean. Mommom loved a clean house. She loved her soap operas just as much. Our routine went something like this: Get up at about 8 a.m., 9 at the latest, clean the house and be done by noon in time to watch the soap operas. *As the World Turns* and *General Hospital* are the two that I can remember best. It's difficult to think that there could be something to clean in a house every day, but Mommom always found something for me and Joyce to be doing. It was bizarre. And Mommom was one of those people who gave the house the white-glove test, so there was no half-stepping on the cleaning.

We also took our turns at the stove. Mommom was a great cook, but she expected us to do our share, and sometimes that meant cooking or at least helping her cook. It was one of the ways I tried to earn my keep.

Joyce's job was to make the mashed potatoes. One time in particular she was at the sink mashing potatoes, which was a big job at our house, with three adults and two children. And Joyce was not a small woman. In order to feed us all, there were a lot of potatoes. So Joyce stood at the sink peeling potatoes and preparing them for mashing.

When we all sat down to eat I tasted the potatoes first. I am not an ungrateful person and I was even a less ungrateful child. I knew that I was supposed to eat what I was given and not make waves about it. Most of the time, I did just that. We ate well, every day. But these potatoes had the distinct pungent flavor of soap. Now, I had never tasted soap, not in any specific way. Sometimes when I washed dishes I got the taste of suds in my mouth. But this was a full-fledged taste of soap. Mommom did not believe me when I announced my findings. In the standard vein of adults in that era I was told to "quit complaining and eat." But I was not about to take another bite of those potatoes. I waited patiently until Mommom had tried hers. The look of sudden dawning was worth the wait.

Mommom hollered into the living room where Joyce usually ate. "Joyce, what'd you do to them potatoes!?"

Joyce didn't sit at the table with us; she had too much girth for the table in the kitchen where we were all sitting. She felt more comfortable in the big red Lazy Boy recliner in the living room where she usually spent time leafing through the Spiegel catalog, *Good Housekeeping*, or the *Ladies Home Journal*. Joyce hollered back, "Potatoes taste fine to me!"

Mommom looked incredulous.

I don't know whether Joyce was just sticking to her story or whether she really didn't know what she had done to those potatoes, but she kept to her story even as Mommom said that she had to eat every bite of mashed potatoes on her plate. We all watched with staggering disbelief.

I've had a theory over the years about what actually happened. There was a very small piece of Ivory soap that was on the kitchen sink. While Joyce was mashing potatoes, the vibration must have made the soap fall into the pot without her seeing it, since the soap and potatoes were the same color. That is the only logical explanation.

But Joyce swore that there was nothing wrong with those potatoes, and absent any real clues to the contrary we just have to assume whatever happened was unintentional. Why she didn't taste the pungent aftertaste of Ivory soap I don't know and I guess I never will. Maybe it was easier to say she didn't taste the soap than to admit something had gone wrong and not knowing what the consequences would be.

We also took turns making sandwiches for lunch. Uncle Pick would come home for lunch and request my sandwiches especially. I still love to cook and I believe that my creativity in the kitchen got its start at Mommom's. I would make the grandest sandwich her groceries would support. Meat piled high, smothered in lettuce, tomato, onion, pickle, cheese, whatever I could get my hands on. I even added seasonings: a little salt, a dash of pepper, oregano. All of it layered delicately between two slices of soft bread. Uncle Pick loved it!

Summers were spent playing kickball in the middle of our street with my friends, Leslie Dewberry, Janette Wilson (who lived a couple of houses down from Leslie), Mitchell Paxton, Wendel Bond, and a few other kids in the neighborhood. Mommom and Uncle Pick's new house was in a cul-de-sac, so the traffic was not a problem. If there were cars that came by, we would just hold up the game until they passed. Mommom, Uncle Pick, Uncle Warren, and Joyce would sit on the front steps or in the screened-in porch and watch us play. Whenever it was my turn to kick, everyone would move way back, because I could kick that ball into oblivion. We loved kickball so much it would be 10 o'clock in the evening, daylight savings time, when we would finally call the game. We wore out a ball almost every week.

Running track was also a love of mine. I was never the fastest girl in school, but I was in the top three. Mitchell Paxton was a Pop Warner track star and my boyfriend at the time. He would run with me around our block to help me build my endurance. I was a 500-yard dash sprinter and I jumped hurdles too. It was not until I was about forty-five years old that I found out I was born with congenital hip dysplasia. I remember seeing a picture of me as a baby with a silver brace going across the bottoms of both shoes to keep my hips rotated correctly. Daddy told me that I had some difficulty walking, but I had no clue what that was all about until I was an adult. Some people used to make fun of how I walked and said I waddled like a duck. Probably still do. I guess with congenital hip dysplasia, I was pretty lucky to be running at all!

When Charles Bentley came into Joyce's life, I was still living with Mommom and Uncle Pick. Everyone was so happy for her. Everybody loved him. He was big, tall, light skinned, had dark straight/curly hair, and was handsome. He was also the father of Joyce's first child, Elyse Charlynne, whom we call Lynne.

I was about twelve and Joyce was about twenty when Lynne was born. I loved helping to take care of her. I changed her cloth diapers (this was before the era of disposables), played with her, fed her, and rocked her to sleep. She loved the mixture of white bread toast with sugar and cinnamon and warm milk pored over that I would fix and feed her. Mommom taught me the recipe.

Lynne's father soon disappeared almost as quickly as he appeared in our lives. He attended Princeton University for a while. Years later, when I was visiting my future husband, who also attended Princeton, I paid an unannounced visit to Charles in his dorm room. Howard's first year there overlapped in time when Charles Bentley was there. Naturally, he was surprised to see me.

We had a short but pleasant visit, while he showed me a color by number he had painted from a picture of Lynne when she was about six or seven years old. After that meeting, I saw him once from afar in the Acme Supermarket that was located on South Governors Avenue in Dover with a new wife, who was White. He either didn't see me or was avoiding me. After that, we never saw him again. Keith, Joyce's second child by her husband Phillip Bryant, came along a bit later. I was not around very much during that time to help out because Joyce had moved out of her parents' home and into her own with her new husband, and I had moved back home with Daddy. How we got back to our old home is quite the tale.

Cousins Keith and Lynne (Joyce's children) Joyce,
Uncle Pick, and Mommom.

By the time I was twelve going on thirteen, Daddy had saved enough money working at Walsh Shoe Repair that he decided to move back to Dover. While we waited for the lease to end for the couple renting our house, Daddy and I both lived at Mommom and Uncle Pick's home. Their new house only had three bedrooms, but there were six of us now. Daddy took up residence in the finished basement. Then Aunt Grace and Uncle Kemp came home from overseas and they lived with us too. That made six adults plus Joyce and I for a total of eight people all living in a three-bedroom house with only one bathroom.

Mommom ran a tight ship and everyone learned to get in, do what you needed to do, and then get out. No leisurely bubble baths here! Having only one bathroom and having it located right off the living room made for some embarrassing moments.

One bright sunny afternoon after church, Mommom was having one of her church ladies meetings. The living room was full of serious-minded women trying to prepare for the upcoming Women's Day program. Daddy needed to use the bathroom. He walked past everyone with a nod as an acknowledgment of their presence. While in the bathroom, he proceeded to make the noises associated with one of nature's calls. As he exited, he could see Mommom's face contorted as if she had just taken a bite of an entire lemon. With a voice of exasperation she exclaimed, "I could hear you!" The ladies group tried to pretend they heard nothing, and with knowing glances at one another continued on with the meeting.

Daddy's response to his sister was with a shrug: "deaf me, noise hear me nothing," as he sauntered slowly past everyone.

It was crowded living space, but it was also fun. Mommom and Uncle Pick were always the ones helping out everyone else. Everyone looked to them in times of need, and Mommom and Uncle Pick never said no to anyone. Eventually, we all moved to our separate homes, but we stayed close. We all would come together and play cards to pass the time.

Their son Charles became divorced and later married his second wife Dorothy, whom everyone called Dot. They bought a house close to Mommom and Uncle Pick's and they would walk down the street to play cards with us too.

There was something about those times when the whole family was together having fun. I had a sense that everything was right with the world. There was noise—good noise—laughter, jostling, joking, an informal picnic. Rules were softened ever so slightly in the name of fun and family. I never wanted those nights to end.

The game of the night was 500 rummy. Daddy added his own special brand of fun by cheating. See, Daddy used to play high school football and at some time during his school days, he broke his pinky finger. It was curled like he was perpetually making fun of the way pretentious people drink their tea. He would take his disjointed finger and use it to hook other people's cards from their spreads if they happened to have a card he needed, or if they were getting too close to winning. Daddy always got caught and no one cut him any slack because he couldn't hear, either. Dot gave a hearty laugh whenever Daddy was up to his mischief. She and Charles seemed to enjoy his antics as much as I did. There was plenty of playful rousting and arguing around his card table manners.

Sometimes cousins Ronnie and Rita would ride down to Dover on Ronnie's motorcycle to visit us. I would beg for a ride and he would oblige my request. At other times, the Wilmington crew and the Philadelphia crew would come to Mommom and Uncle Pick's house during the summers. I loved when the whole family would get together to share food and catch up on the latest news. On a few occasions, Aunt Gertrude, who lived in Philly, would bring her daughters Delores and Joyce (also called

Bunny) and Ronnie and Madge (his first wife) would bring their sons, Ronnie Jr. and Tony. (Later Ronnie would divorce Madge and marry a second time.)

He and his second wife, Bertha (affectionately known as Bert), would then bring their son Derek, whom we call Spanky, to the family gatherings. Ronnie also had a daughter, Lynn, but I didn't meet her until I was an adult. Ronnie, Rita, Roma, and Roma's husband Paul Roberts, who was hard of hearing, brought their two sons, Paul and Darryl, who were also hard of hearing, with them. Rita brought her daughter, Tawanda. Not everyone came at the same time, but there was always a crowd.

The end of our time at Mommom and Uncle Pick's was bittersweet. Daddy and I had been used to doing our own thing and living our own lives a few years before, but we had both grown accustomed to the busyness of living in a house with so many people. Plus, Daddy was trying to

Ronnie and Bert.

save so that we could have some money of our own like we had before he had to close the shop. He didn't want to reopen Mosley's Shoe Hospital, so he found work with a local shoe repair shop and began working with Gregory Hardgrove, the owner. I called him Mr. Gregory.

One night, however, Daddy and Mommom got into it. I don't know what it all was about. I was still kind of young to be too involved in grown folks' business. But Daddy needed me to interpret for him, so a lot of times I got to hear things I was probably too young to really need to know anything about.

The argument got heated and Daddy resorted to his favorite phrase "son of a bitch" when somebody made him mad. My fingers were flying as furiously as their emotions and then Daddy signed something else. I won't say what it was out of respect for both of them, but it was enough to make my eyes widen with concern and surprise. And then Mommom turned her angry gaze at me, who should never have been in the room in the first place, and said, "What'd he say?!"

For me that moment defined my struggle for those last few years. Mommom had been my guardian and protector, but Daddy was Daddy. If I told Mommom what he'd signed, it was a betrayal of Daddy's and my relationship. If I refused to tell her what he'd signed then I was nothing but the interloper I had fought feeling like for so long. All of these feelings jockeyed for place in the split second I had to put them in perspective. Mommom was waiting. . . .

Daddy and I moved out a few days later. We weren't quite as ready as he'd have liked us to be, but we were as ready as we were going to get. Mommom didn't like being called such names and certainly wasn't going to let someone call her one in her own home.

PART 3

Too Big For My Britches

WHEN DADDY AND I LEFT MOMMOM AND UNCLE PICK'S, I was nearing the beginning of my teenage years and it was the middle of the sixties, which Walter Cronkite said were the most turbulent years of the decade, or something like that. He was talking about Vietnam, race riots, the sexual revolution, and antiwar demonstrations. I was talking about life with Daddy. I remember those years of turbulence and appreciate having lived through them and emerging pretty much unscathed.

Daddy and I were caught in an ugly dance. The scene at Mommom's epitomized the experience. In a lot of ways I felt I was the caretaker in my family. I could move through our society without Daddy, but he, although capable, had more ease when I was around. After all, he had raised me as a single male Deaf parent in the fifties. I think he would have rather had the comfort of quick communication than to go back to the struggle of using paper and pencil writing everything down; not being sure if he understood the other person and if he was understood by that person. Who wouldn't?

On the flipside, Daddy had to relinquish a lot of privacy as well. I'm sure it wasn't any easier for him to have to share things with me most parents wouldn't feel comfortable with revealing to their children. But we were all each other had.

Still it caused no end of drama. It made my teen years probably worse than most average teens with two parents who could hear. It was difficult to separate myself from Daddy. I knew he needed me. And I think we both felt a profound sense of abandonment at my mother's leaving that we couldn't quite articulate, even years later. It wasn't her per se as much as what her leaving represented to us. We bonded in her absence.

Me and Dad.

I was the one Daddy came home to. I was the one who heard his troubles at work with Mr. Gregory at the end of the day. And sometimes I just did not want to be the one. At thirteen years old, though, the story's all about you and that's how I felt. I loved Daddy, but that's a heavy burden for a child to have to carry. I'm sure he didn't mean to lay his troubles at my feet and he wouldn't have if he'd known just how much it unnerved me. But what would that have done to him? I could communicate my frustrations to others. I didn't even realize how much it unnerved me until much later in life and I got to sit back and look at my teenage years from the slightly more objective lens of my adult years.

While working for Mr. Gregory, Daddy was frustrated most of the time. Mr. Gregory, who I personally had no gripe with, and whom I have grown to love over the years, was White and he was the boss, which meant that right or wrong, whatever he said went. That alone gave Daddy enough fodder to go on for months. But to add insult to injury, Daddy was an excellent shoe repairman and business man and it upset him when he saw and experienced things that he felt Mr. Gregory could have handled better.

Daddy would see Mr. Gregory talking to the customers longer than he felt was necessary. Mr. Gregory should have, according to Daddy, been putting in more time repairing shoes than flapping his gums. Daddy felt overburdened with the lion's share of the work and yet Mr. Gregory was getting all the praise from customers for the fabulous end product.

Previously, Daddy and Mr. Gregory had been competitive colleagues. But now, with Daddy's business having been sold, he and Mr. Gregory had to work together. I'm sure Mr. Gregory knew that. It might even have contributed in some small way to the frustration Daddy felt at the decisions Mr. Gregory made on the job. Still, Daddy had learned to live with that. Or at least he'd tried to learn to live with that. Daddy was an outspoken man and it was difficult for a man who had been independent at a time when most Black people were making their living at the behest of others to have to bend to the decisions of someone else. Daddy had been truly blessed up to this point in our lives and I'm sure he knew it. And if he didn't know it he knew it by the time he got through dealing with Mr. Gregory's antics.

There was no yelling to someone to get their attention if they were not close by no matter how inappropriate it might be, no matter who your parents are, or what their personal difficulties might be. If I wanted something from Daddy or he wanted something from me, we had to have face-to-face contact or at least be within "hand" shot. A lot of times I had to be where Daddy was just for practical reasons that don't occur in the lives of most teenagers. My sense of loyalty to Daddy had created a difficult dependence that I was anxious to break just a little bit by the time my personal life became important to me.

My frustrations were mounting by the day. I had my own issues to deal with. Boys were becoming increasingly relevant to me. What to wear was always a challenge. Miniskirts were in. Uncle Pick used to say, "Careful Jeanie, if you bend over, people are gonna see everything you had for dinner last night." I would just give him a look. Being cool was the objective 24/7. I did not have time to listen to, worry about, or try to solve the problems of my father who—as far as I was concerned—was old enough to handle his own problems.

When I was in the seventh grade, I recall one of my school bus drivers. He was an off-duty White policeman who knew my Dad. He showed up at Mommom's house to talk to her one day after a verbal altercation I'd had with him after school. He said or did something that rubbed me and my friends the wrong way and I, with my sass, was the only one left standing after everyone else had common sense enough to back down and leave. I thought he had come to tell her about the altercation and that I was going to be in big trouble. Apparently, he had told her about a summer camp for teens my age that wasn't too far—about an hour's drive away. I'm sure the altercation was mentioned, but I had no idea how this was going to end. Well, I ended up going to the camp with my best friend, Wilma.

I had never been to a summer camp before and it was great! Most kids would have felt like it was a punishment of some sort, considering the circumstances under which my family found out about the camp, but not me. Although I was nervous as this was a new experience and I had no idea of what to expect, it was time to be a kid. It provided me time away from minding grown folks' business and having to deal with grown folks' emotions. I was free to be thirteen!

We had cabins to sleep in, but one night, I remember making a bed of pine needles, covering them with a blanket and sleeping out under the stars with the other campers for the first (and only) time in my life. We played games, sang songs, roasted marshmallows, and told stories over a campfire. I had so much fun! When it was time to get back on the bus at the end of the week, I shed a tear. I would miss the people I had met and the fun I had. It was back to Dover with nothing to do.

I don't remember that officer's name, but I would like to thank him for seeing something in me worth working with. As a White man in a racially charged time, he could have done any number of things to inhibit my progress. Instead, he chose to see the "me" that was lurking under all the anger and frustration. That was the first intervention I remember. Others were yet to come. I hadn't reached the peak of my troubled teen years yet.

Looking back, there were so many people that had their eye on me that I wasn't even aware of. They just showed up in my life. The saying "It takes a village to raise a child" was certainly true in my case. Growing up in a small town where everyone knows everyone else can be a pain, but can also give you a sense of belonging to something greater than yourself. Being the child of a single father brought out the maternal instincts in a few women, but none of them could be a full-time mom.

In the middle of all this, my mother came back to visit. Why she chose this time was never clear to me. She never explained where she had been or why she left. So we just spent the week together getting to know one another on a superficial level. I had been told that she was coming and I had anticipated her arrival to some degree. I think I was driven by my curiosity to see what she looked like and if I looked anything like her. I had always thought I looked like my dad. Instead, I discovered that I looked just like her. Sure, I had a lighter complexion and straighter hair like my dad, but I looked like her.

I hadn't spent a lot of time tracking her whereabouts, but I'd heard things. I knew she had spent some time in New York and then Baltimore. I had no idea how she spent her time or how long she ever spent in any one place. I didn't know if she thought maybe she'd made a mistake and wanted to get back with my dad. I was about as interested in her reasons as I was in my father's constant complaints about Mr. Gregory. Still, she was my mother.

I remember she gave me a pretty necklace, suitable for a thirteen-year-old. There were no particular markings on it that made it stand out in my mind. I just remember its specialness to me because it was the only gift I had where I could say, "My mom gave me this."

We would go for walks around the neighborhood and the boys would wolf whistle at my mother. It wasn't enough that she up and left with no apparent warning, that she returned basically the same way, and that I was having a halting relationship at best with my own mother, I had to endure the fact that boys also found her *hot*. My emotions were caught in a tornado of hate, anger, pride, and hope. I just didn't know what to do with her. So, I didn't do anything. I rode the wave of her arrival like I did everything else. And at the end of the week, she was gone . . . again.

Fun Times

BY THE MID-1960S, I WAS IN FULL-FLEDGED ADOLESCENT mode, attitude and all. The Civil Rights movement was in full swing, although its appearance in Dover was introverted at best. We got whisperings of it from around the country, but Dover didn't experience it the way other parts of the country did. There were no riots or burnings. Although Daddy would continue to engage me in discussions about the political scene, as a teenager, I wasn't terribly interested in being socially conscious. My world was being shaped by Motown.

Music had always been a big part of my world. The music from radio and TV filled my quiet world and something about the beats and rhythms had an effect on me. Martha and the Vandellas, The Supremes, The Temptations, Smokey Robinson and The Miracles, Marvin Gaye, Mary Wells, and Stevie Wonder dominated the music scene.

The Motown sound was gaining momentum and Philadelphia was evolving as a city with its own sense of musical style. Our proximity to a city so rich in musical history had its impact. James Brown and Aretha Franklin were powerful voices that everyone was trying to emulate. Before school, Leslie, Janette, and I would meet at Leslie's house and play music and practice our dance steps so when we got to school we'd be the ones in the know about what was cool. We'd get so caught up in practicing we'd have to run to the corner before the school bus left us.

There was not much for teens to do after school. I had outgrown my love of making mud pies, so mostly I watched TV, although the selection wasn't anywhere near what it is today. *Gunsmoke*, Mitch Miller, Liberace, Red Buttons, soap operas, and *I Love Lucy* occupied a good deal of my TV time in the 1960s, as did *Peyton Place*. At the time, Philadelphia aired a music/dance show called the *Discophonic Scene*. It was hosted by Jerry

Blavat, "the Geator with the Heater," a popular local DJ. My friends and I never missed the show.

My world on the outside, even without my mother, looked a lot like the world of any other young girl, growing up in the fifties and sixties on the Mason-Dixon Line. I was surrounded by friends and family. Dover's Black community was small and insular, mostly by necessity; so, while I didn't know every Black person in Dover, I knew enough people to probably connect me with every other Black person in Dover. I went to church, did some things I probably shouldn't have, got caught sometimes, and sometimes got away with stuff.

During the summers, Black folks swam at either Dover's Silver Lake, Lewes, or Rosedale Beach. Carr's and Sparrows Beach in Maryland were also popular places for African Americans. Silver Lake was pretty dirty, but it's what we had. Families packed their picnic baskets, grabbed their blankets and bathing suits, and headed for the water. There was also Rehoboth Beach for White people, which was located about forty-five minutes south of Dover.

Nanticoke Indians went to Rosedale Beach located in Millsboro, Delaware, along the Indian River. Rosedale Beach was named after Dale and Rose Street, who purchased the property from Noah Harmon. Rosedale Beach Hotel and Resort operated from 1925 until the 1970s. It began primarily as a church organization called Harmon's Park that evolved into a place for people of color to go for entertainment during segregation after the Streets sold it to a Philadelphian. It had a board-walk, hotel, campground and picnic area, dance hall, and an amusement park. It was a hub for top entertainers of the day such as Cab Calloway, Ella Fitzgerald, Count Basie, Lionel Hampton, Aretha Franklin, James Brown, Stevie Wonder, and Jackie Wilson. After integration, visits to the facilities declined. In 1962, a storm destroyed the boardwalk, which was never replaced.

Downtown's main thoroughfare was Loockerman Street, which is what Forest Street became after you crossed the railroad tracks and rounded the bend. When I was a young child, Daddy and I used to walk together from our home hand in hand the entire length shopping for whatever we needed. I loved the way my hand felt in his. It gave me a sense of security. I could feel Daddy's love for me through the vibrations of his touch. He would always put me on the inside as he protected me from the cars that drove past sometimes splashing rain water that had settled alongside the curb. As a teen, I walked alone or with my friends going to purchase toiletries and other necessities. The image of Daddy and I making that trek would pop up in my head every now and then. Downtown had small quaint shops on either side: clothing, hardware, shoes, a local five-and-dime store, F. W. Woolworth, a gift shop, and some other stores. South Governors Avenue was also a main street that ran perpendicular to Loockerman. Right across from Mr. Gregory's shoe repair shop was a bakery. The Acme Supermarket was a few doors down from Mr. Gregory's on the same side. Next door to the shoe repair shop was a small restaurant where Daddy and I would order delicious cheeseburgers to bring home for a weekend treat. It was a welcome break from the usual fare of food such as something in a can called "three steak," three round patties of mystery meat and gravy in each can. Corn, green beans, and sliced *to*matoes, as Daddy pronounced it with the accent on the first syllable, were great sides.

The few restaurants we had were nice sit down places before fast food joints practically took over Route 13, the main highway going through Delaware. In the early days, Black people were not often welcome in the nice restaurants, so until fast food restaurants began appearing on Route 13, we ate at home. The first fast food restaurants that I remember were Hardies and Gino's (similar to McDonalds). Then there was the park and eat style restaurant where you could drive up in your car, park, and the car hops would come out of the restaurant to your car to take your order and then bring it out to you as soon as it was prepared.

Just like the balcony in the theater, we didn't really find our segregation from the nicer restaurants to be a big problem. On a Saturday or Sunday morning, waking up to the smell of fresh brewing coffee, eggs, toast, apple sauce, and scrapple cooking on the stove was better than any restaurant where you weren't wanted in the first place.

I did not know until I moved away as a young adult that people outside of Delaware and the mid-Atlantic states did not know about scrapple. Scrapple is a pork product introduced by the Pennsylvania Dutch community that comes in a block, like Spam, that you slice and fry. Delicious!

Then there was Dover Air Force Base. Some of the Dover girls viewed the base and getting to know the airmen that came in and out of the area as a form of entertainment. They would go to some of the dances that occurred on the base. Other girls viewed Delaware State College in the same vein (college boys instead of airmen) and would attend the dances that were offered on campus. Some girls went to both. I went to the base with my girlfriends a few times, but I much preferred the college scene.

Then there were the town boys. Clearly our entertainment options were limited.

When we heard that Dover had plans to open a teen disco, we knew that would be our new hangout. The Count Down was owned, I believe, by the brother of one of my friends with whom I had played kickball in my younger years. It was above an adult lounge and we had to climb nearly to heaven to get to the top. But once we did, oh boy! They played all the most recent music and once they even brought in Jerry Blavat, "The Geator with the Heater" as a guest host! It was such a blast to see him in person.

The club was a good hangout, but not everyone appreciated it. There were fights and other disturbances until finally the club closed down not long after it opened. But for a brief moment, Dover could call itself hip.

I Am More Than My Hair

AT ABOUT THIRTEEN, MY BEST FRIEND AT THAT TIME, Yvonne, attended summer school. Summers in Dover back then were sleepy, if that's not trite and cliché. Not much happened any time of the year, but in summer, the eastern sun kicks up pretty bright and pretty early. Most of the time we kids just drifted and made our own fun. Yvonne and I were similar in build in that we were small and could fit into each other's clothes. She wore her hair short and had an endearing round face.

One day Yvonne invited me to go to summer school with her, and as a testament to how "sleepy" Dover is in the summer, I agreed! And, of course I wanted to look cute. Now, I already had relatively long and wavy hair. Why I felt the need to put a hair piece on is something at this point in my life that escapes me completely. I'm sure it made perfect sense to me then as senseless things always do to a thirteen year old. I can only imagine that I had been indelibly marked by the ostentatious styles of Diana Ross and those wonderful falls she wore in performance. I don't even remember where I would have gotten such a thing. I guess you could say it was a precursor to the weaves that women wear today. Anyway, for whatever reason, I thought I needed the piece. I put it on and I went to school with Yvonne, thinking I was cute.

When the day was over, we headed out of the building and started toward home. We weren't the only ones on the street that day, there were some other girls and boys walking along and we were all doing what kids do, chatting and being silly.

Nobody saw the car until it was on us. First, the car sort of brushed by one of the girls walking behind us. The car didn't hit her really, it kind of brushed her, close enough to touch, but not enough to knock her down. That dubious distinction was saved for yours truly.

A responsible driver would have stopped to make sure the girl was okay. He should have stopped, but he didn't and I was right in his line of fire. In a moment that was eerily similar to the fatal accident that took my grandmother, the car hit me and knocked me down, sending my hair piece flying in one direction and me in the other.

Now, no one knew I was wearing a hair piece. As I said, my natural hair was long so the long piece probably didn't set off any alarms with my friends. So, when the hairpiece went flying everybody was in a thither about my hair. From my spot on the ground, I could hear the buzz about whether or not my natural hair was still actually on my head.

"Oh no," my friends said. "Her hair has come off her head, it's like she's been scalped!"

The driver of the car did stop that time, long enough to pick me up and put me in the backseat and drive me to the hospital. By this time, Dover had just integrated and there was no need to stop at the doctor's office first. I was okay enough to give him a piece of my mind all the way there, too. I don't remember everything I said, but I'm certain that it wasn't ladylike. I told him what I thought of his driving skills, too. By the time we got to the hospital he probably wished he had left me back there on the ground with my hair.

At the hospital they gave me a good going over and sent me to Mommom's house. I'm not sure how I ended up there as my father and I no longer lived there, but Daddy was at work and there was nobody at home. But Mommom was always the one that everyone went to when they needed looking after.

Later that day, the driver's father came by. He was a preacher at one of the churches in Dover, not one that I attended. He came bearing the biggest fruit basket I'd ever seen. My guess in hindsight is that he was afraid we were going to sue, but we weren't that kind of people. I was all right and there was no serious harm done. But the fruit was good.

Apparently, the minister's son had taken his father's car without his permission. To top it all off, the boy didn't even know how to drive (and I don't mean that in the cynical sense, although it certainly applies). He literally did not have a license to drive.

I still have the scar on my back, though, a reminder of how easily other people's decisions can have an impact on the lives of others, both positive and negative.

Integration

TECHNICALLY, DOVER HIGH SCHOOL WAS INTEGRATED IN 1954 just after the Brown vs. Board of Education ruled that the separate but equal decision was unconstitutional. However, Black and White students did not suddenly begin to attend school together. Nor did they suddenly begin to *want* to, at least not in Dover. The few Black students that initially integrated the previously all-White Dover High that year were carefully chosen. For the most part, segregated schools still existed until 1965.

Booker T. Washington Elementary School, where I started in 1959, was segregated from its opening in 1922. That one school housed grades one through six. From there, students attended William Henry High School from grades seven through twelve. As luck would have it, they instituted full integration the year I was supposed to attend William Henry High. At the end of my sixth-grade year, we were suddenly told that instead of going to William Henry, we would be attending a newly organized Central Middle School for grade seven. Grade eight would be located at William Henry, but it would now be known as a middle school. From there, we would attend Dover High School starting with grade nine. Today, I and many of my friends still regret not having the opportunity to attend William Henry when it was a high school. It was something that we had looked forward to our entire grade-school years.

That first year at the predominately White middle and high school, some of the Black students (me being one of them) did not always feel at home. In this instance, I didn't want to be there, nor did I feel I was wanted by some. There weren't a lot of racial incidences, but that didn't mean much. There was discomfort emanating from both sides.

Many of the Black kids wanted to be at the all Black school they had planned to attend. A few of the White kids I'm sure wanted us to go there too. But we managed. A number of White students, however, embraced us and culminated friendships that would last a lifetime. At Dover High there were also many teachers that stood out as being encouraging and helpful.

One of my best Black friends in high school, Beverly Fairley, went successfully for some of the extracurricular activities like cheerleading, where she was the first Black person to do so, and the Yearbook Club.

I kept with my other friends. I felt that if I tried to fit in with the White social life at Dover High, some of the Black kids would think I was trying to be White. If I hung around my Black friends exclusively, I would miss the socializing that might have made integration a little easier to bear. I'm sure it was one of the reasons as a teenager I became disengaged with school. After having academic success in my earlier years, I developed a rebellious streak my first three years in that integrated setting. My last year at Dover High, however, I matured a bit and had a change of heart.

With the support of my friends—Jackie Brown, Beverly Fairley, Wilma Harris, Cynthia Edmonds, and Linda Reed—I decided that I would run for Homecoming Queen. It would be the first time a Black student would compete. I was one of five girls that entered into the competition. It would also be the first time that the homecoming committee changed the voting rules. Typically, the student body would select one of several candidates as their choice. The year I decided to run, however, each student was required to vote for two candidates. It would have been impossible for me to win. I guess the status quo wasn't quite ready yet to have a Black Homecoming Queen. I came in fourth. Nevertheless, it was a great experience that taught me much about perseverance in the face of obstacles. I got to ride in my own homecoming float (a decorated car) and had my picture with the other girls in the local newspaper, the *Delaware State News*. Daddy was not so much a part of this aspect of my life and he didn't say much about what I had accomplished. I guess he was still trying to figure it all out. It was a new chapter for both of us.

In some ways the mentality of Delaware can be a southern one. And in the 60s that meant resistance to integration. Back then, Black people went to the same schools, churches, and social functions. There wasn't a lot of racial violence in Dover. Blacks and Whites had an amiable relationship. It was a very comfortable "don't bother us and we won't bother you" experience.

Growing up, I was aware of racism in that way that many people experience it, from the news or in magazine articles. My family story is filled with moments flavored with the national racist mood. As a child and even as an adult, though, I didn't understand how those moments had any effect on me. They were simply things that had happened, like having to sit in the balcony of the theater.

There was a value to going to school with people who looked and thought and acted like me. Black Dover was a relatively tight-knit community. It was nice to know that my teachers were close, they knew my father, and cared about all of us. The early integration experience was intimidating and caused much anxiety, suspicion, and mistrust. White people seemed accepting of the fact that they were to attend school with African Americans and vice versa. Everybody thought this was something everyone in the Black community wanted. What we wanted was equality, to be able to go anywhere we wanted and to do anything we could conceive. During that time, separate was never the problem as far as I was concerned. Just like those in other cultures, we had our own schools, restaurants, hotels, and other businesses. There was a cohesiveness and there was love and affection for one another.

Black folks generally lived on the west side of the downtown area except for a housing development called Capital Green. The other areas were Lincoln Park, Simon Circle, and West Dover Heights. People typically kept their homes clean, grass cut, and cars in good repair. They were proud of what they had, worked hard, and took great care in all they did. There were a few "drunks" that limited their hangout near the "beer garden" (that's what we called the local bar) but they were the minority.

Like any other place, Dover changed over time and became a small city, more urban. It still only has a one street downtown, but other areas have developed, and along with that came the issues every city deals with.

There is no way to avoid the inscription of the past onto your experience. I learned that the hard way, which I suspect, is the way everybody must learn it. I fought it. I wanted my own path in life, one that I could say was mine alone without the encumbrances of history. But The Great Spirit, The Creator, The All, God, had other plans.

Hanging Out

I LOVED BOYS. MY BEST FRIEND LOVED BOYS TOO. I WILL never forget the adventures Yvonne and I had. Eventually we went our separate ways, but we have continued to periodically stay in touch over the years. I made new friends as I grew up, but Yvonne helped me walk the tightrope of independence I longed for during that difficult age.

I lived as close to the edge as a teenager in Dover, Delaware, in the 1960s can live and not fall to the dark side. Occasionally, I crossed that line. I was cute and I had a father who trusted me, worse yet, who *had* to trust me—a definite formula for trouble, especially when you mix in the desire to assert independence.

I drank, but I did not smoke or do drugs. I like to kid myself into thinking that Daddy didn't know what was going on. He never let on that he knew, so as a petulant teenager, I was able to kid myself a long time. But looking back, I think he probably knew. There wasn't a lot he could do. And he might also have been a little skeptical about confronting me because we both knew he needed me.

I had another boyfriend by this age. In my thirteen-year-old way I'm sure I loved him, though now, the thought of what my life would have been if we'd followed through with our plans to marry makes me tremble. Dad was sure I was headed for trouble with him and he was right.

Drinking and boys at the age of thirteen is a lethal combination. Nothing good can come from that. He was eighteen, much too old to be dealing with the likes of me. But there wasn't a lot to do in Dover and, eventually, trouble will find anyone. I became promiscuous at that early age. At the time it didn't matter to me. I was in love.

There were no at-home pregnancy tests then and going to the doctor was out of the question. But I had missed two periods and I had been having sex. I was pregnant and didn't know what to do. We had actually planned to get married when I got older, even before any of that happened. I even wore a small diamond engagement ring that he had given me. When I showed it to my dad, he just shook his head in disbelief.

No one had ever talked to me about the girlie things. When my cycle started at the age of twelve, my cousin Joyce was given the edict from Mommom to take me to the store and get me some pads. That was the extent of any conversation anyone had with me about what girls my age should know. The only reason I knew I was supposed to have a cycle was because I'd had a health class in school. My father certainly wasn't planning to have that conversation with me, and the women in my life just didn't talk about such things. Whatever I knew about the world of sex I got from school and friends. The clinical version of things cannot prepare you for the stark reality of the dangers of sex at that age.

I was terrified, but I had no idea where to turn or who to turn to. I could not imagine telling my father. Telling Mommom would be tantamount to suicide, although deep down I knew that if I carried the baby to term, sooner or later they would have to know. My girlfriends were supportive. They tried to turn me on to what turned out to be innocuous potions and things they'd heard would help me out of my predicament. I tried them, but nothing happened. I went about my life after I realized I was pregnant doing exactly what I'd always done. My social activities didn't change. I continued drinking, went to gym class regularly where we made pyramids and fell all over ourselves, and ate whatever I wanted. All of that contributed to what happened next.

By this time I had a birthday and had turned fourteen. And I began bleeding profusely. I was at home when the bleeding started. I figured I had to tell someone. I had lost a tremendous amount of blood and was growing weaker by the hour. I told Daddy that I thought I needed to go to the hospital. When I got there the doctors knew right away what the problem was and they admitted me immediately.

I was not there when they told my family what had happened, but I know they were told. When I was ready to come home, Daddy never said a word. Everybody else in my life had something to say. I can't tell you how many times I heard, "You're gonna be just like your mother!" behind that episode. The negativity just kept coming.

But Daddy, what I remember about him during that period was that as I lay in the bed recovering physically and emotionally, he just rubbed my back and said nothing. Our private language had failed us. I had disappointed Daddy. And that was worse than anything anybody had ever spoken in words to me about it.

The look on his face told me everything he couldn't say. When I looked at Daddy I saw every fear he had for me reflected back. I'm sure he blamed himself as much as if not more than I blamed myself. I did not want to disappoint him, and in that moment I understood that my actions had consequences. I had breached our private bond. The emotional chasm between us was out in the open now. I had been deliberately operating in a language my father could not understand.

My dad's answer for his fears realized was to remove the phone, which, as far as he could tell, was the conduit for my behavior. My life revolved around the phone. Whenever he saw me at home I had the phone wrapped around my ear and, shortly after, I would hang up and leave the house. Because Daddy couldn't hear what I was saying and I wouldn't tell, he had to determine what I might be up to by other means. My attitude didn't give him any comfort.

In hindsight, I think a big part of my problem was, other than being a teen, I had never been just a child. From the age of five, I was into adult business in a most detrimental way. My emotional and mental maturity was required. So, I guess I thought that my body and mind were in the same place. I took care of Daddy. I did a lot of the cooking and the cleaning. I answered the phone when it rang and couldn't hand it over to Daddy. When he had important business to handle, it was my business too. How could I not come to the conclusion that Daddy and I were equals? How could I not believe that I didn't have to answer to anyone? My self-esteem, whether I believed it then or not, took a hit from my mother's abandonment.

But Rome, as they say, was not built in a day. My attitude did not change overnight, miscarriage or not. I wanted to put that episode behind me as quickly as I could, so I did. As far as I was concerned it was a bad moment like when you trip and fall in front of a cute boy. It was easier to move on and not think about it. By not confronting it, helped me to not change.

Once Daddy removed the phone we had to go back to relying on the neighbors for phone calls. Today that kind of thing would be inconceivable. I don't know many neighbors who would tolerate letting someone else have their phone number for that reason. Every time someone called for me one of the neighbor's daughters would come and get me.

One time I remember having a falling out with Daddy about something, the topic of which I no longer remember. I went to my bedroom, shut the door, and began screaming at the top of my lungs. That was one of the few luxuries I had that many of my friends did not. Once I shut my door I was free to rant and rave to my heart's content. I must have gone on for about ten minutes.

After I calmed down I opened the door and my neighbor was standing there. I nearly died with embarrassment. She looked like she was ready to die from embarrassment, too, to be honest. I got defensive immediately.

"What are you doing in the middle of my living room?" I snapped.

She looked terrified, but I was unyielding. She had caught me in the middle of a private rant.

"I just came to tell you that you have a phone call," she said.

I felt awful, just awful. Here they were doing me a huge favor and I was being hateful.

Still, Daddy wouldn't get the phone back so Yvonne and I had to make our plans over the phone at my neighbor's. I would tell Daddy I was going out. In Dover there aren't many places to go without a car, which is probably why he never seemed to get too worked up about what I might be doing.

The lesson here is that teenagers can always find trouble. In the middle of nowhere with not another human being in sight, teenagers can find trouble if they're really looking for it. Now, Yvonne and I didn't go out looking for trouble, not consciously. We weren't that type, really. We were looking for fun. But trouble can wear some funny disguises and fun is one of its favorites. We were having as much fun as we could get away with.

It was not unusual for us to wander up the main road until someone was going where we wanted to be. The things I did to get where I wanted to go would terrify a parent today. I suspect if my father had known he would have been terrified even then. Yvonne and I would basically flag down a car that we thought might be going toward the roller rink or wherever we thought we wanted to be and hop in. Because we all knew each other, it wasn't like getting into a car with a complete stranger. Yvonne and I had places to go and things to prove to ourselves and our parents. We, of course, knew it all, and on top of that we were indestructible. You absolutely cannot argue with fourteen.

The one consistent thing there was to do in Dover was roller-skating on Tuesday nights. That was the night the local roller rink played Black music. The rest of the days the roller rink belonged to the Whites. But on Tuesdays we could bring our own records and the DJ would spin all the Motown hits all night. My favorite was Junior Walker and The All Stars' "Shotgun." All the best music of the sixties propelled us around the rink. I used to try to skate to keep up with the cute (and fast skater) Roger Boone. Roger had two brothers, Jim and Derrick, who were also attractive. All the girls liked the Boone boys. Skating around with our group of friends was like those nights at Mommom's where the family got together to play cards. We could just be ourselves.

The roller rink was a good distance from our house, and often Yvonne and I had no idea how we were going to get to the roller rink to participate in this love fest. All we knew was that we were going. And when we got there, which we always did, we often had no idea how we were getting home. Yet somehow we always managed.

We would get to the roller rink and absorb the culture congregating there, virtually writhing in the sense of freedom we had afforded ourselves. Patting ourselves on the back for our cleverness at eluding our incompetent parental units. I got to sidestep responsibility for one night a week and be a kid, or what I thought was a kid. I got to flirt with the boys, drink and socialize with my girlfriends, listen to a little Marvin Gaye and Martha and The Vandellas, and let go of Mr. Gregory and Daddy and whatever else might be trying to bring me down. Before long I glided through the rink forward and fast, letting the music take me.

If it wasn't Tuesday, I had to find other ways to amuse myself. One night Yvonne and I ended up at a party back in a shack, somewhere I had no business being at my age. It was the kind of party adults talk about in hushed whispers and nobody of any quality ever admits to having been. Loud music and even louder people have the walls shaking as soon as the sun goes down. Liquor is the fuel that keeps the fires going. It is inevitable at these kinds of parties that somebody will remember a long ago wrong and let it come burbling to the surface with the force of a hurricane.

When the shooting started, I left. I don't even know how I got home that night. Yvonne and I knew we didn't belong there, and as wild as we wanted to be we also knew we had better not be found there by the police. Nothing can clear a room like the earsplitting pop of gunfire. Every available exit was bursting with bodies. I went out a window. What else can you expect from a place called The Gun and Rod?

Mrs. Parker

EVERY SUCCESS STORY HAS A MRS. PARKER IN IT. SHE IS the woman in the community who takes an interest in some at-risk teen and turns her life around. In my life, Mrs. Parker deserves some credit in trying to help me find myself outside of the negative influences that seemed to be beckoning me to the dark side.

Mrs. Parker, a middle-class Black woman with a coffee complexion, was the dietician for the now reconfigured William Henry Middle School, which I attended. She and her husband lived in one of the nicer subdivisions down the street from Mommom's house. The Parkers didn't have any children. A woman with her own children has scant time to be worrying about someone else's ill-behaved child.

As I mentioned previously, in Dover, all of the Black people lived together. It didn't matter whether you had three college degrees or none. We were bound by our singular description of Black. Doctors, lawyers, teachers, and handymen all lived and loved in the same general community. Whatever was happening to the children in the community was happening to the entire community.

Mrs. Parker was a very nice woman and her intentions were that of any concerned community citizen. Apparently Mrs. Parker saw something salvageable in me that she thought she could reach. She had taken on a monstrous task to try and tame me. She and her husband were of the college-educated variety of Blacks who saw their role in the community as one who could uplift. She spoke in crisp, no-nonsense English. When she spoke, you could hear the vowels struggling to maintain a straight military line. It is almost impossible to imagine her in anything wrinkled, worn, or old.

When I started high school, she hired me to help her keep her house dirt free. My tasks were simple. She wanted me to do chores around her house after school and to get her dinner started before she came home from work. The goal, I believe, was to keep me off the streets and away from alcohol and the other unsavory influences in my life. I wonder sometimes what she saw in me that she didn't see in others that caused her to trust me in her house and with her things. I wonder why she thought I was responsible. I was the epitome of the wild child. By the time Mrs. Parker got to me, I had had sex, been drunk, gotten pregnant, and had a miscarriage. I had lived through things many grown-ups don't even experience.

But I think she knew. Black Dover was too small for her not to have known. I didn't realize that at the time. I thought secrets were secrets and that what you didn't want people to know they didn't know. But she must have known what I'd been up to. And like Daddy, she didn't judge me for my mistakes.

It's funny to look back and think about how others saw me at that difficult period in my life. Did the adults who knew me understand my situation? Did they just feel sorry for me? Did they give me the benefit of the doubt because they knew my father, aunts, and uncles and knew their good name? I don't lose sleep at night wondering about it, but it crosses my mind periodically that this woman allowed a kid who clearly did not fit the image of little Miss Sweet and Innocent to come into her home when no one was there.

Luckily for Mrs. Parker, I had learned how to clean a house extremely well from Mommom, the Queen of Clean, and got plenty experience doing it for her and at home with Daddy. I had enough home training to know that regardless of what I did with my friends, there were rules about the respect for others. The line there was clear and unimpeachable. In other words, I knew how to keep my ill-conceived behavior under the radar.

Mr. and Mrs. Parker's house was always clean, even before I came to clean it. Everything was as neat and spotless as they both were. I would quickly go home from high school, eat a snack, watch as much as I could of the popular soap opera *Dark Shadows* and then leave in order to get to work on time, and make the fifteen-minute walk to Mrs. Parker's house.

I usually arrived at 4 p.m., worked two hours, and left at 6 p.m. She always had a list of chores that she left for me to do on the counter in the kitchen. The list, written in pencil, explained everything she expected to be done that day such as changing the sheets on the beds, scrubbing the kitchen floor, dusting, vacuuming, and hand washing her stockings as well as other items. There was always something different to do each day.

After I had completed my cleaning and just before she was to arrive home, I was to begin preparing what she had asked for that evening's dinner. One of the dishes I prepared involved slicing white potatoes with onions and sautéing them in the pan and then placing baked pork chops on top so that the drippings from the chops would fall onto the potatoes for seasoning.

Sometimes, Mr. Parker would arrive home first. I don't remember what he did for a living but he always wore a suit and tie. He would spend time in the kitchen ironing his white shirt for the next day while I was cooking and setting their table. Mr. Parker with his caramel complexion was tall with a medium build. He was very laid back and said very little beyond his daily greeting.

"Hello Jeanie, how are you today?"

"I'm good," I would reply.

"Dinner sure smells good, what are we having tonight?"

He always seemed happy with whatever my response would be. At every meal there was to be a napkin placed under the fork, which I learned should be placed on the left side of the plate. The sharp edge of the knife always faced inward on the right side of the plate and the spoon was to be placed on the outside of the knife. At home, we never used napkins for everyday meals. If you needed to wipe your mouth, you just got up from the table to get a paper towel.

Upon Mrs. Parker's arrival, she and I would discuss how the cleaning or cooking went that day before it was time for me to leave. If I didn't do something to her liking, she would explain to me in her quiet refined manner how it was to be done. I would promise to get it right the next time and I did. She would ask me how things were going in school. I was always a good student, so no dramatics there. Sometimes we talked about my predecessors, girls who had previously held my position and what they had been doing after they left her employment.

Every Friday, she would leave my remuneration of $10.00 for the week's work under the list. It was good, honest money. I held that job for four years. I honestly have to say that Mrs. Parker did not keep me from wandering the streets, drinking alcohol, or having fun with my friends. That lesson had to come at my own pace and in my own time.

I had a savings account that was opened for me in 1960 when I was in the second grade. My teacher Miss Mildred Weston had someone to come in from Farmer's Bank to talk to the class about the importance of saving money. That day, each student received an account with their very own dark blue savings account passbook to record their deposit of twenty-five cents. What forethought my teacher had! I kept that account until I married and moved away from Dover in 1978.

Miss Weston was a quintessential teacher, just like every teacher I had at Booker T., from first grade through the sixth—Mrs. Blanche Hickerson, Miss Mildred Weston, Mrs. Dorothy George, Mrs. Marjorie Fisher, Mrs. Mildred Bedford, and Mrs. Lola Tue. They all treated us as if we were their very own children. They accepted no nonsense, but expressed love, care, and concern for every student. Just as importantly, we all loved them.

Who I am today can be credited to not only those teachers, but also the only two principals I had: Mr. S. Marcellus Blackburn and Mr. Wesley Hall, and the secretary, Mrs. Helen Hicks. The entire school, including the custodian, was like family. Years later, they changed the name of Booker T. Washington Elementary School to West Dover Elementary School (perhaps to be more politically correct). In more recent years, Mr. Wallace Hicks, Mrs. Helen Hicks' husband, and my friend Regan's father, got a committee together to successfully change the name once again back to its original historically significant and most fitting name.

Because of the lessons about the importance of saving from Miss Weston and Daddy's frugal nature having grown up in the Depression era, I was very good about saving the money that I earned from Mrs. Parker and used it wisely to purchase things I needed such as toiletries, new clothes, stockings, and the like. Daddy always provided the basic essentials, but I learned early on that a girl needed her own funds for the extras. I will say that the experience at Mrs. Parker's also contributed to who I eventually became and for that I am forever grateful.

Although Mrs. Parker didn't impact me immediately, when I was ready to grow up and take responsibility for my life and actions, part of what helped me do that was the unyielding example she set for me just by being herself. She was different from other women I knew. Watching her conduct herself in such a sophisticated manner was a lesson in and of itself.

Time for Change

THERE ARE FEW THINGS THAT CAN MAKE A TEENAGE GIRL hell-bent on self-destruction (at least metaphorically) straighten up and fly right. A nice boy is one of them.

For me it was Howard. Don't get the idea that the moment we saw each other I made the decision right then and there to begin living my life right. Far from it. From my perspective, Howard was so different from the other guys that, at first, he was more a curiosity. Most of the young men in Dover were headed straight for life in Dover. Their plans didn't extend beyond the Kent county line.

But Howard wasn't from Dover. He was from Cincinnati, Ohio. He was eighteen years old and came to Dover to attend Delaware State. While in college, Howard lived with his grandmother Lillian Johns, whom everyone called Tim because she was tall and slim like a tree. I guess Tim was short for timber. Howard was average height but appeared much taller because he was so thin and wore an Afro that was larger than he was.

This was 1968 when the Afro hairstyle was all the rage. I even tried to wear one by rolling up my fairly straight hair on small Lilt rollers every night before bed. In the morning, I would take the rollers out, use a pick to fluff out my hair and be ready for the world. The only problem was that my 'do would only last until about noon. It would begin to droop and lay flat to my head. After that, I looked like a hot mess.

The first time I met Howard, I thought he was a nerd (when the term was considered a negative). I was used to boys who moved fast and who liked girls who were like lightning, so he didn't register on my radar as someone I thought I would eventually marry. Howard came from an established family. They were college educated with high expectations of themselves and the people they dealt with. His father was a dentist who had his own practice, and his mother graduated from Delaware State and later earned her master's degree. She taught home economics at a Cincinnati high school.

Today, his oldest sister Lillian Hall Hawkins now has her PhD. His younger sister Juanita Hall Gaines is an MD. My brothers-in-law, Lonnie C. Hawkins, Jr. and Fred Gaines, have a JD and a master's in counseling, respectively. Then there is nephew Samuel Gaines, who has a BA in social work. Niece Tiffany Gaines Holland has an MD. Niece Lauren Hawkins and nephew Lawrence C. Hawkins, III, have their JDs. My oldest daughter Ilea Hall Speight has her Master's in social work, her husband has a BA in IT. My youngest daughter Karelle is currently working on her PhD in anthropology. I have a PhD and Howard has two doctorate degrees, a PhD in experimental psychology and a PsyD in clinical psychology. This is such a rare occurrence in one family.

Howard's parents met when his father came to Dover to do his residency with Dr. Charles Williams, the dentist that lived a few doors down from Mommom and Uncle Pick when they lived on Queen Street and whose office was located directly across the street. Uncle Pick used to clean Dr. Charles's office after he came home from working at the NeHi bottling plant every evening. Uncle Pick would take me with him to help out.

At fifteen years of age, I wasn't afraid of much. I was moving fast, but I really wasn't going anywhere. Not in Dover, anyway. And I wasn't fast enough to be thinking about getting out of Dover.

By then, though, I was beginning to migrate to a new group of friends. Yvonne and I were going our separate ways, as sometimes happens. I won't say I was learning to behave myself, I was just learning new things to get into. I started hanging out with Jackie Brown, Linda Reed. Sometimes Beverly Fairley, Cynthia Edmonds, and Dessie Wright would be with us—all friends from Booker T. that I had known since first grade, except for Cynthia who was a military kid that joined us in our senior year at Dover High.

Jackie was a key person in this crew because she had a car! She turned sixteen before the rest of us, so she had the wheels to take us to paradise. She would drive her father's old 1953 tan, four-door Ford. Jackie would make the rounds and come by our homes to pick us up. Some of the town guys would meet up with us and buy us alcohol as we were too young to get it ourselves. I'm not sure how we or they managed not to get into any trouble with the law or into any serious accidents. Jackie had that gregarious personality that everyone looked to. She drew our attention with her humorous antics and was the life of any party. Walking down the halls at Dover High, she and I used to pass a threaded needle through our pierced ears to connect ourselves. We were lucky we didn't pull our ears off!

I don't know why Daddy trusted me the way that he did. Maybe he felt he had to. He'd seen me at my worst. Maybe he figured there was no way to put the toothpaste back in the tube. Plus, it was quite easy to turn him off if I wanted to. I simply needed to turn my back and communication between us was impossible. If I left the house, he had no way to call my friends and find out where I was, and their parents couldn't call him. We didn't have texting then.

Distance only absolved me of the responsibility of having to justify my whereabouts. I couldn't call him, and the other adults in my life seemed not to concern themselves with where I was or what I was doing at that time. I was Daddy's responsibility. Maybe they didn't know. He had taken the phone away, but that hadn't stopped much. I don't think he knew what else to do, but hope this phase passed on its own.

I shudder to think of it now, how we were playing a dangerous game, but of course, at the time we didn't think about that. We'd ride around Dover and if there was a dance at Delaware State at Delaware Hall or the Student Center, we'd spend time with the college crowd. We loved to dance with the college boys. I would sometimes see Howard there and have a dance or two with him, but that was it. For Howard though, he said he was charmed with me and my short dresses from the very beginning. It's a good thing he would have the patience of Job.

My friends and I hung out afterwards in the parking lot, each of us talking to our favorite guy. Jackie liked a guy by the name of Brandon Nigh, Dessie liked Victor Warner, and I was enamored with Bobby Lima who was part Cape Verdean. His father was also one of the famous Tuskegee Airmen that fought in World War II. Linda was dating Christian Haverly, a guy stationed at Dover Air Force Base. She didn't much care for the college type. Beverly was dating a local guy from town, Johnny Cedars, and like Linda, was not as interested in the Del State guys. Cynthia was interested in one guy in particular from the Base and ended up marring him after high school. I remember thinking how brave she was to pack up and move to a foreign country she had never been to before. But all this did not happen before Jackie and I had a chance to influence her to hang out with us, drinking vodka and orange soda—our version of a screwdriver.

After our parking lot trysts, we'd be starving, so we'd go across Highway 13 to Gino's for burgers and fries. After that, the girls and I would ride around town till the early morning hours laughing, giggling, and stopping along the way whenever we saw someone we knew. At the end of our merriment, Jackie would drop us all off and the plan was on again for the following weekend.

When we weren't hanging out at Del State, Jackie would come by and we'd just hang out at my house. In addition to the college guys, there were also town boys that we liked, so they would come, park in my driveway or in front of my house, or take us for rides. Chris Talbert with his '56 Chevy, Jim Moses with his '59 Chevy, and Brian Wilcox with his '68 GTO all had cool cars that spent time parked in my driveway.

Once Jackie's mom, Thelma Brown, came by. I think she suspected something unladylike was going on at my house. Whatever she saw that day, she did not like. It was a while before Jackie was over to my house again. She felt these boys were too old for us to be hanging out with. We found out later that she'd had a talk with a guy's mother and told her to keep her son away from Jackie. At the time, that seemed like a ridiculous thing to do. But now, I wish someone had been there to do that for me.

Somewhere in all of this, there was the tall White guy that had the cool Camaro. He and I hung out for a bit. We went down to the Harrington Fair—a staple summer attraction—along with my friend Beverly and another Black guy. My friend was the only White person in our group. I remember an African American passing us and saying to me in a tone of disgust, "Huh, I thought you were one of us." I ignored their comment, walked away with a roll of my eyes, and had great fun at the fair.

But, life would never have been this much fun without Jackie Brown and her dad, Bud Brown's, hooptie.

You might think that all of these experiences taught me some lessons, but I didn't get it until I failed a final exam in high school because I had been under the influence. I had always been a good student and had never failed anything until that point. My behavior had been predominately social. Now it was something else altogether. This was a public failure, something that could be documented in the community, something that couldn't be relegated to rumor. It was definitely time for a change.

She's Back

AFTER HER FIRST VISIT TO DOVER WHEN I WAS THIRTEEN, my mother moved to Baltimore, after having left New York. Living closer now, she would come to visit me more regularly during the summers. Once, when I was about fifteen or sixteen, she brought with her three of the four other children she had birthed after she left my father and me— Chuckie, Jeff, and Julian.

I remember my dad being upset that she had brought the boys with her. All of the boys carried his last name and not the name of their true fathers, which caused my dad much pain and grief. I was upset too. My thinking went something like this: My mother had come to visit me and here she was dragging along these three kids that I had never before met.

It was bad enough she had abandoned me and that I was carrying the weight of that betrayal in everything I said and did around Dover, the least she could do when she came to see me was let me have her undivided attention. Plus, I had to confront the fact that these boys got to be with her all the time (so I thought) and I only got piecemeal handouts of her time.

The moments of my life swirled around me as I contemplated the wonderful life they were living without me. When she brought her other children all I could think was: *Why not me?* What did I do that I wasn't the one she wanted to keep? Every bad decision I ever made came with that emotional baggage.

I later found out that things were not as they seemed. Apparently, she had decided to leave the three boys when they were young with their aunt to raise when she lived in New York. Turns out the stories that rattle around in our head oftentimes are just that—stories.

So Daddy and I were both stressed, but for different reasons. I was very loyal to my dad and felt the pain he felt. My best friend Jackie

135

happened to be across the street with her dad at my cousin Sylvia's and Cousin George Hackett's house when my mom arrived at my house. Cousin Sylvia, a slender woman, was noted for being an all-around good cook, but the chicken and dumplings and the fabulous sweet rolls she baked were legendary. Jackie did her best as my friend to comfort me and be a listening ear.

My mom and the boys were only around for a few days. They would spend their days visiting with other relatives in Dover and their nights at Aunt Emma's. For a few days, they came to my house. We just walked around the streets of Dover, or sat around. The boys I recall were much more active than anything I had ever seen. They were constantly running and jumping on and off things and flushing stuff down the toilet. After the week was over, Daddy and I sighed a bit of relief and went back to our usual routine.

Those boys are of course now grown and mature men with their own families. I haven't seen them in a very long time, but we manage to stay in touch via Facebook. Julian now resides in California with his beautiful wife and gorgeous daughters. The oldest of the four boys, Tommy, who had lived with my grandparents in Clairton, moved to California in his adult years and has since passed away. Jeff is also living in California currently with his beautiful companion. Chuckie now lives in another state. I admire each of them for their strength, courage, and endurance.

PART 4

Building Confidence

MY COUSIN JOYCE HAD A CHILDHOOD FRIEND, GLORIA Morris, who had a full-size personality to match her full-size figure. When they were teens, Gloria, her sister, her brother, and Joyce formed a singing group called The Morris Singers. They traveled the local church scene singing gospel music. Although Joyce was not a Morris, she was received into the group as if she was a member of their family.

Later, Gloria became Rev. Gloria Morris. She married Johnny Snipes and added his last name to hers. Gloria started and directed the first Gospel choir at Whatcoat United Methodist Church, which was the oldest African American church in Dover and where I had been a regular member since the day I was christened as a baby. This was quite an accomplishment because, heretofore, Whatcoat had an adult choir that, shall we say, sang more of the sleep-inducing hymns sung in the drier Methodist tradition. Members of the choir were not professionals, but did their best to sing to the glory of God. They typically got a wince or two from me.

As I look back, I can see that the youth gospel choir must have been a divinely inspired way of helping me find the right direction. I joined because I loved to sing. I stayed for so many more reasons.

It was something to do and it was something I loved to do. I was never told officially that I had a good singing voice. I'm sure I sang for family and friends, but they were not the kind to point out things like that. They would surly tell you if you were doing something wrong, but it was seen as promoting vanity to tell you that you were good at something.

But one time, my friends and I were backstage behind the closed curtains at our high school for a program, where the choir was to sing a selection or two. I, along with my friends Beverly and Jackie, were members of the choir. While the audience filed in, popular music blasted from the sound system and it was a tune I liked, so I began to belt out the song. Suddenly, I heard a voice from in front of the curtain. One of students in the audience asked in a tone of voice that showed they were impressed with my rendition, "Who is *that*???" Then they implied that I should keep singing. My friend Jackie quipped, "Girlfriend, don't let that go to your head." But at that point I understood something else about how other people perceived me. I could sing and sing well. So the church gospel choir seemed like a good choice when the opportunity presented itself.

I knew Gloria (that's what we all called her) and most of the kids in the choir, so socializing wasn't a problem. And of course there was Howard, even though at the time I had no idea the impact he would have on my life. Because his grandmother attended Whatcoat, she brought him to church with her. It was discovered by Rev. Gloria that Howard was an accomplished piano player and was interested in becoming the gospel choir's pianist.

Back in Cincinnati, Howard had his own jazz group, The Jazz Casinos, which played at the local bars and clubs around Cincinnati and across the river in Kentucky. Once, while the group was playing a gig in a Kentucky jazz club, a union man came up to them during their break and asked their ages and to see their music union card. Of course, they were too young and didn't have a card, but the music was thoroughly enjoyed by all the club patrons. Afterwards, they packed up their gear and headed back home to Cincinnati after being exposed.

I went to choir rehearsals every Wednesday evening and performed with the group all weekend at other churches in the general vicinity and then back to Whatcoat on Sunday. It kept me out of a lot of trouble, I'm sure of that. When the group traveled, we would travel by car caravan. Howard drove his car and I slid into the front seat and made myself at home. The front seat of a guy's car is a position of power for a girl. It's like marking territory. Not just any woman gets to occupy that seat. Regardless of how I thought I felt about Howard or what I told him I felt about him, I didn't want anybody else occupying that seat. Plus, it was a really cool car: a cherry red 1969 Mustang!

We often followed Gloria's car, which wasn't easy because she drove like a madwoman. It was not unusual to watch her weave through traffic like a NASCAR driver, or, if you will, a bat out of Hell, crossing lanes and generally making traffic bow to her demands. It was an amazing thing to watch. Her motto was, "I've got Jesus and that's enough." We all prayed a lot to make sure.

The choir was a self-esteem boost for me like no other. When I opened my mouth, all the sound in the world convened in my voice. I felt invincible when I sang. Songs like "How I Got Over" and "Somebody Bigger Than You And I" were two of my favorites to sing.

Howard's grandmother had probably warned him to steer clear of me. I wasn't the worst kid in Dover. I went to church on Sunday and I was respectful, but I had a history. I don't know how many people knew all there was to know, but what they didn't know their minds shaped and molded like clay until it fit the rest of the picture. I can hear tongues clucking now about how he should "stay away from that Mosley girl."

My mother's reputation from having left my father had stained me as well. Her rebellious act of up and leaving her husband and child behind hadn't endeared her to the stalwart, powerful women in this matriarchal community. My presence only reminded them that there had been a defector in their midst. They were worried, I think, that the apple didn't fall too far from the tree, that I would not be able to sustain a role as a respected woman in this community.

I started realizing, though, even with the negative whispers that life was pretty much whatever I wanted it to be. Problem was I had no idea what I wanted life to be. I wasn't thinking about college. No one in my family had ever been and had never mentioned the prospect of college to me. Even with Delaware State College practically in my backyard, it was still a distant place.

I assumed I would graduate high school and become a secretary or an office manager, do something functional. I would take my place among the adults in Dover, find my niche, and get in it. In my family, functional was what paid the bills. College was for other people, rich people, girls who didn't get themselves pregnant at the tender age of thirteen.

However, just like Mrs. Parker, Howard saw something in me that even I hadn't thought existed. I suspect that I was drawn to the intellectual nature in Howard. I believe that I was being led to him. The events of my life seemed so random at the time, but in putting them together to look at the coherent whole, it is obvious that there were larger forces at work than either of our individual wants or needs could accomplish alone.

He was patient. I was young. At fifteen years old, there was little he could do with me as a conscientious eighteen-year-old young man. So he waited. He would spend time trying to learn a bit of American Sign Language so that he could communicate with Daddy. Daddy, however, had no patience with Howard's snail-paced communication and would always resort to asking me in an exasperated tone, "Say he what?!"

Still, I had no discernible interest in Howard at first, besides his '69 Mustang. He found excuses to come to my house and stay for hours. It started with him bringing me home from Wednesday night choir practice. I was used to walking home, although the walk from my house to Whatcoat was not too much of a haul, maybe a half a mile, maybe more. Howard offered to drive me and I saw no reason to say no.

Then he'd have some other excuse for coming by my house. Sometimes he just wanted to see what I was doing. My dad was always there and Howard would often have dinner with us. I was a great cook even at that age. I had lots of practice. We would sit on my couch and talk. We talked about lots of things. And somewhere in our discussions Howard said, "Where are you planning to go to college?" It was the first time anybody had said "college" to me in a way that presumed I would be going.

As I said, Howard comes from a line of college-educated people. College was not something he thought about as an if/maybe proposition. He never got to waffle over the decision of whether he would go. It was always assumed that he would. The only question mark on the landscape of his post–high school education was *where* he would go. He took the same approach with me. I don't think it ever crossed his mind that I hadn't considered the possibility. In Howard's world *everyone* considered the possibility.

At first, I looked at him like he'd lost his mind. Howard might as well have been asking me to fund a trip to the moon. Hadn't he seen my surroundings? My family didn't have those kinds of resources. My dad made a living fixing peoples shoes. We ate every day, but the cost of college wasn't figured into his savings budget. No one else in my family had ever been to college.

I said in my most exasperated voice, "Where am I supposed to get the money to do something like that?"

Howard didn't blink. "We can find the money," he said with all the confidence I needed to make me want this.

The idea settled so easily in my mind and made itself at home that I couldn't believe it hadn't crossed my mind before. All of the cynicism of my early teen years melted away almost instantaneously. I believed he could do what he said he'd do. The glimmer of an idea bloomed into a full-fledged decision to make it happen, if for no other reason than to prove to Howard that I could do it. I didn't know then that I didn't have anything to prove to him; he already knew that I could do it.

The Power of Support

HOWARD AND I DIDN'T BECOME OFFICIALLY A COUPLE until three years later when I was eighteen years old and he was almost ready to graduate from Delaware State with a bachelor's degree in psychology. We had the college conversation, but it didn't become a reality to me until I realized that I was actually going to go to college. *Me.* The girl who had herself become occasional grist for the town gossip mill and who had always thought of college as something other people did. This girl was going to college!

So, in the fall semester of 1971, it happened! It was through no small effort on Daddy's or Howard's part either. First, there were applications to fill out. We didn't have much money, so I only filled out one application to Delaware State College. Then there were funds to secure. Once Daddy realized that I wanted to go, he was on board with it. He and I went to the bank and I interpreted the conversation that went on between him and the bank associate.

"How may I help you?"

"My dad wants to get a loan to help pay for me to go to college," I voiced.

This was one of the many ways in which my interpreting for Daddy occurred in those days. Daddy and I would have a conversation beforehand about what he wanted and then I would handle the transaction, explaining to him what was going on. If he had input he wanted to give or if they needed information from him, he would respond. Of course, today, a professional interpreter would make sure that the Deaf person is the one in charge of the situation.

Daddy was able to obtain a loan for approximately $1,000. I don't remember if that was the entire sum the bank was willing to give him, or if that was the amount Daddy was comfortable with taking on. Either way, we walked out of the bank with enough funds to get me started on my new adventure. Back then, if you were an in-state student, the tuition was somewhere around four hundred dollars a semester plus fees and books.

The magnitude of this event for me was indescribable. Delaware State was on the outskirts of Dover both physically and mentally. It was a place I went to for parties with my girlfriends Beverly, Cynthia, Linda, Dessie, and Jackie. I had lived my life with the expectation of joining an office pool and settling into Dover adult life. Now, I cannot imagine what I thought I was going to do there. But I must have had some idea because no other option seemed logical to me until Howard mentioned college to me the first time.

My best friend at that time, Beverly Fairley, came from a background like my own, which many would think precluded any talk of college. Her circumstances were different, but the outcome was basically the same. We were the girls, either because of where we lived or who our parents were (or were not), that others did not expect to succeed.

Looking back, it seems that our lives were not terribly charmed, at least not in that way that feels good right away. Both of us were very much products of our circumstances. The word *victim* leaves too much margin for error. I was on my way to becoming a victim and Beverly could just as easily have given in to the negative influences and the environment that surrounded her daily.

But like me, she was able to go to college and continue on to earn a PhD with the support of her family and friends. Unfortunately, she passed away April 7, 2000, at the age of forty-seven, from a bizarre virus that attacked her heart. Within a couple of days, she went from being healthy and talking with me on the phone, to making her transition a few days later. Beverly left a legacy of courage and strength of which her family and friends can be proud.

What caused us to move past who we were then to become who we are today? Some people will argue that we had angels who helped us and that those angels no longer exist in our society. I would agree that we had help. Everybody has help. Anyone who suggests they achieved any kind of success without the help of others is delusional. Still, there is more to it than that.

I believed I could do it because somebody, Howard, told me I could. No one had openly expressed that kind of faith in me before. My family had no notion of the kind of life Howard was introducing me to, a life of possibilities beyond Dover. They were pragmatic people and, although they probably understood that college was a good thing, they did not see it as a real choice for anyone they knew.

But, I reached back to my grandmother. She didn't know that her Deaf son—my father—could go to school until somebody told her he could. And when she knew that there was something for him out there to make his life better, she ground in her heels, pushed up her sleeves, and pushed until the doors of PSD opened for my father.

I had to be open to the voices trying to get through to me. I had to want it for myself as badly as anybody else wanted it for me. The formula didn't work as long as I tried to keep myself an X factor, separate from the voices. When I allowed myself to want what others knew I already had in me, I became unstoppable.

I believe that my father, my family, Howard, Rev. Gloria and the Gospel choir, Mrs. Parker, my teachers, and many others who I may or may not have known about that had a hand in my development were all a part of divine intervention.

College Girl

BETWEEN HOWARD AND HIS CONTACTS AT DELAWARE State, they wrangled me a scholarship in the music department. I didn't really appreciate the parameters of my obligation, which was to sing in the college choir, but at the time, I didn't really know enough about how these things worked. I was going to college. I was about to do something no one in my entire family had ever done. When I told everyone I was going to college, my Uncle Pick with his dry, down home sense of humor said, "Well, Jeanie done jumped up and got smart on us."

I lived at home through my college years. Dad and I pretty much lived our lives like we always had. Because of that, I found it difficult to get into the rhythm of traditional college life. I did my work, but I didn't have the opportunity to experience dorm life and really immerse myself in the campus experience because I lived at home.

I hated to admit it then, but it was rather frustrating. College is a time when you are developing your adult self, separate from your parents. My father's reliance on me made that challenging. A particular example involves my desire to pledge a sorority. Both Beverly, who attended Bowie State, and Wilma, at Delaware State, had pledged Alpha Kappa Alpha Sorority, Inc. (AKA) in their sophomore year. Many of the professional women in Dover were members of AKA and so it was only natural that I'd expect this to become a part of my life.

But once you accepted that offer from the sorority, there are a host of other things you need to do and you needed to be on campus to do them. You are no longer a single *one* but a member of a unit that operates as one. There were activities which required the attendance of every pledge. For the girls living on campus, that was okay. They could pair up and walk back to the dorms together. Most of what we did occurred on campus, which made things simple if you lived there. I, on the other hand, still had to drive home.

Daddy was another obstacle. He didn't understand college life. He believed that college was school, a place to learn from books. He didn't understand that learning can happen in many different ways. When I took the car and was gone for hours, he'd worry and fret and sometimes be mad. I had to be cognizant of his work schedule because we only had one car.

Trying to live the life of the stereotypical coed became nearly impossible. I had to drop the line. It was one of the toughest decisions I ever had to make. Joining AKA made me feel like part of something that was outside of my usual life in Dover and it was a good feeling. I didn't want to let go of the sisterhood bonds that were forming, but the stress and anxiety of the lifestyle was taking its toll. I knew that for my own best interest, this was the best course of action. I had been an excellent pledge and I knew that when I reviewed my life years down the line, Alpha Kappa Alpha Sorority, Inc. would somehow be a part of it.

By 1973, Howard had already graduated from Delaware State and given the student speech at his graduation. He would come down to Dover from Princeton where he was working on his PhD when he had time, and sometimes when he didn't.

I plowed through my school work, burying my frustration in the interest of papers and exams. School had never been difficult for me and I found college no different. I still liked to have fun, but I knew when and where to draw the line. There was no point in being in college if I wasn't going to graduate. Besides, I also knew I was carrying the weight of expectation on my shoulders . . . and not the good kind.

It would not have surprised me either then or now to find that there were a few people who not only didn't think I could follow through on this experience, but who had probably taken bets on just when I would crash and burn. Not so much because I am me, but Dover is a small town and so it's easier to stand out. I am sure there were many people watching me who wanted me to succeed as much as I wanted me to succeed. But somehow it's the negative voices that usually get into our heads and wreak the most havoc.

So, I did my work, was a conscientious student and got through the first year. My grades were stellar, social life was working fine, and things, it seemed, were changing for me. It turns out though, that my satisfaction was a bit premature.

I got a letter from the bursar telling me that I had lost my scholarship, in short because I had failed to participate in the regular choir. I had joined the college's gospel choir, skillfully and with great style, directed by the White brothers. I loved singing with all the gospel choir members. Nobody told me that in order to receive the scholarship I had to participate in the regular choir! If somebody had mentioned that, I would have been there too, with bells on. Now I was on the horns of a true dilemma.

What was I going to do? I'd already had a taste of what I could do and have and I didn't want to give it up on a technicality. I cannot describe to you the fear that washed over me at the thought that I would not be able to return to Delaware State. The things I had been exposed to, the knowledge I had absorbed about myself and the world, where would it come from if I didn't get to come back here?

I was frantic. I was a goner. The choir of negativity in my head cleared its collective throat and began warming up to sing my failure.

The way I saw it, I had two options. I could let this be the end of my career at Delaware State, take it as a sign that it just wasn't supposed to be, and go on home and try something else. Or, I could figure out how to keep myself where I knew I belonged. I was ready for the fight. I was prepared to beg, plead, and do whatever was necessary to keep myself on this path.

To this day I have no idea how the money that materialized into my account got there, but when I went to the financial aid office to work out the plan, there was extra money from various scholarships in my account. There was a roundabout explanation about scholarships and corporate money from Playtex, which had its headquarters in Dover, but it never quite made sense to me. And, honestly, as long as it meant I didn't have to get off the road I was on I didn't really much care. The money was there and I could return to school.

The cold sweat that had been my perpetual companion during this ordeal dried up and I felt a weight the size of Dover lift from my shoulders.

Divine intervention? Maybe. Probably. I have to look at the moments of my life and ask myself the hard questions. I don't know what would have happened to me if I hadn't been able to return to college. Perhaps I'd have gone on and fulfilled that ambition in the secretarial pool. Perhaps not. Perhaps that failed opportunity would have confirmed for me the price of misplaced ambition. Perhaps the negative voices in my head would have had a field day on my failure and my path might have been bumpier than even the one I imagined.

What I do know is that college had opened up for me a whole world of possibilities I had never been able to consider. I felt my expectations of myself lift with my spirit and I believed that the world could be mine. I no longer saw life through the narrow lens provided by my small, hometown life. At Delaware State I met students from all over the country, the world, and from all walks of life. People were there to become all sorts of things: doctors, lawyers, teachers, nurses, and scientists, just everything! I learned that financial resources and bad decisions were not necessarily the determining factor in how your life turned out. I learned that partying is fun, but there are other ways to make life interesting. I understood a little of how Daddy must have felt once he'd got the hang of life at PSD.

But, even though I had the whole world at my disposal, I still didn't quite know what that meant. I stayed where I was comfortable and focused on business classes. I think I did it because that was the track I was on in high school and, absent any real advice about how to plan my college life, I stuck with what I knew was working. I just wanted a degree. Nothing in my life had prepared me for a life after college. I did not have plans for a major career in corporate America. When I look back I realize how little I knew about what I was supposed to be doing.

I certainly didn't know my life experience could be applied to a career. No one told me that my life with Deaf parents was something unique or that my ability to use American Sign Language was something the world desperately needed. I was about the only person I knew with Deaf parents, but it had been a part of my existence for always, so I never thought of it as *different* in that way that might make it relevant beyond me. I never had cause to use ASL with anyone outside the family except for Daddy's few friends, so while in some place I probably knew that others used it, the idea of it was just that. An idea. It wasn't like Spanish or French or German. Not to me, anyway. It was just how I communicated with Daddy.

I didn't know right away that I could take my life and make it mean something to the world. I still had some lessons to learn first.

To College and Beyond

BEVERLY WAS AT BOWIE STATE IN MARYLAND JUST UNDER a couple of hours away. Dessie Wright and Wilma Harris, my very first childhood friend, were at Delaware State with me. Wilma lived right behind Mommom and Uncle Pick, but she never socially hung out with me and my group of friends when we were teens. She was the little Miss Sweetie Pie who never got into trouble or did anything she wasn't supposed to. Attending college together gave us a second chance to rekindle our friendship. We attended some classes together and ate in the Student Center cafeteria with some of the new friends we made. Those 4 years seemed to fly by and graduation was looming on the horizon.

Graduating from college was going to be a big enough project for me. I had pushed my way through lost scholarships, an aborted attempt to belong to something bigger than myself, and classes whose value beyond student torture I couldn't always figure out. Now Howard was talking to me about graduate school! Who did he think I was? Didn't he understand that college was enough? I had done what no one thought I could do, what no one had considered I should even *try* to do. Isn't this where most people stopped? What was one supposed to do once she had accomplished the impossible? Apparently, according to Howard, she was supposed to apply to graduate school. So I did.

The process wasn't that simple. I mean, the decision to do it was. I try not to think about how random my decisions were back then, but essentially I trusted Howard. And if the next step was graduate school, well then, that's what I was going to have to do. But still, I had no idea what graduate school meant for me.

As I said, up to this point, I had no idea that being the daughter of Deaf parents made me special or that I could fill a niche that had gone pretty much ignored. But when I heard that Western Maryland College (now known as McDaniel College) had a graduate program in Deaf Education, I didn't see how I could pass that up.

In order to be eligible for admission into Western Maryland, I had to pick up a psychology and a sociology class. To do so, I enrolled in summer school at Delaware State right after I had just graduated with my bachelor's degree.

While I was running around trying to get my ducks in a row for graduate school, I had completely forgotten the real implications of my future plans. I would be leaving Dad for the first time in our lives. I tried to see things logically. He had left me when it had been necessary. I'd had to live with Mommom and her family while he'd worked in Wilmington. This would be a lot like that, I convinced myself.

But I hadn't quite wrapped my mind around the realities of the situation. I did not want to deal with the fact that this was bigger than anything we'd done so far. When Daddy left, I was literally his little girl. Now I was a grown woman. I was not leaving on a temporary basis to return and have things go back to the way they had been. When I left, I would return an independent adult. Daddy, I think, knew this and it bothered him.

We were a team. Each of us had something the other needed and now I was expressing that I didn't need what he had anymore. A part of me will always need Dad, but I think he saw a part of our lives coming to an abrupt and definite end and for him it was scary. Who would make sure he was understood when it was critical? Who would make sure he understood? Those were things I'd always done.

The guilt wore me out. I struggled with my decision even after I got to Western Maryland. I had always been Daddy's support. Was it selfish of me to leave him like this? Did I owe him my life?

The drive down was the worst. Howard and I were in the front seat of Howard's car, which was now a black Oldsmobile Cutlass Supreme and Daddy had taken his place (literally and figuratively) in the backseat. Every now and again I would look back and Daddy looked so sad. I know he was happy for me. I was the first person in the family to go to college. A graduate degree was a horse of a different color all together. Of course he was proud of me.

After we arrived at my dorm residence, Daddy and Howard unloaded all my stuff and helped me move in. Then came the inevitable. It was time for both of them to make the trek back to Dover. On the way back, Daddy, now in the front seat, turned to watch me wave goodbye. It was one of the toughest moments of my life. He just kept staring out that back window with the saddest face I have ever seen until I couldn't see him or the car any longer. I don't know how long I cried that evening, but I do know that even to this day that image will forever be seared into my memory.

To pay my way through graduate school, I had secured a job as Head Resident in the women's dorm for undergraduates and the Total Communication House where both Deaf and hearing graduate students lived that came to Western Maryland College to obtain their master's degrees in Deaf Education. My job was to patrol the halls, make sure rules were being followed, and dorm restrictions were not being ignored. At the beginning and end of every semester, I would dole out and retrieve room keys. If a lightbulb needed replacing, it was my job to contact maintenance. I was allowed one weekend off a month. I always went to see Daddy.

On my first trip back home, Howard came to Maryland to pick me up. Once home, Daddy and I went to the Pontiac dealership where Daddy purchased my first car, a green and white Aspen. I was thrilled to have my very own car! He knew I needed transportation to get around school and to travel back and forth. By that time, he had sold his Pontiac and never purchased another car. He signed to me, "car mine, old, drive don't need. Dover small, walk all around can me."

Another month would pass before I could return home to check on Daddy. There was no phone for me to call him and see how he was doing. I would have to call Mommom to get any report. I couldn't wait to tell Daddy how things were going for me. We hadn't seen each other in weeks. I knew he couldn't wait to see me either. It would be like old times if only for a weekend.

I pulled into the driveway to find a *For Rent* sign plastered on the front of the porch. I stepped out of the car uncertain about the state of things, my joy and excitement on hold until further notice. When I got in the house Daddy confirmed that he had placed my room up for rent. The hurt in his action was physical. He might as well have stood me up naked in the center of town and slapped me silly. Daddy was trying to rent my room. He was putting me out. How could he do this to me? Why would he do this to me? Where was I supposed to stay when I came home to visit?

In his defense, he never followed through with renting the room. I suspect that the sign was his way of both getting back at me for trying to have a life outside of him and to solidify for both of us the turn our relationship had taken. Daddy knew that even if I came home after graduation, it would never be the life we had built. Our memories had built a beautiful house of cards for him which had come tumbling down without warning. The avalanche must have been devastating for him to hurt me like that.

Miracles Do Come True

IN 1976, STEVIE WONDER HAD RELEASED HIS 18TH ALBUM "Songs in the Key of Life" with Motown, and I had finished grad school and obtained my M.Ed in Deaf Education. I was able to complete the degree in one year because I tested out of taking the required sign language courses.

Little did I know at the time, but when I was in my last year and ready to graduate from Delaware State in 1975, Congress passed Public Law 94-142, the Handicapped Children's Act, which guaranteed children with disabilities the right to a public education. I don't even remember if I was aware that such a law was coming down the pike, but it was and it was going to have a tremendous impact on the rest of my life. Finding a job after graduate school wasn't as difficult as I thought it would be. Delaware was in desperate need of teachers who could communicate with deaf-blind students who were in segregated facilities as well as those being integrated into the regular public school system due to the act.

I was hired immediately before the ink had dried on my diploma, as an itinerant teacher with the Margaret S. Sterck School for the Deaf in Newark, Delaware (now known as The Delaware School for the Deaf).

My job was to visit the schools where they had placed children who were classified as deaf-blind in classrooms with children that had other disabilities or in mainstream classrooms with typically functioning students. I was to make sure they were getting needed services. My home base was Sterck, but I was basically all over the state providing services to children with disabilities and their families. This meant I spent a great deal of time on the road with the Bee Gees and Yvonne Elliman as my close companions.

The Sterck School has an interesting history. The school is named after Margaret Sterck who was the first teacher for Deaf students in Delaware.

She opened her home in Wilmington in 1929 for that very purpose. She funded the school entirely through private support.

In 1945, the state mandated funds for educating Deaf pupils who were sent either to Wilmington public schools or to the Pennsylvania School for the Deaf, where my dad went. In the mid-1960s, though, the Pennsylvania School for the Deaf didn't have any more room for Delaware students, so the state had to figure out other options. They built their own school in 1968 and named it in honor of Margaret Sterck. It opened its doors to the first students in 1969.

Overall, I enjoyed my job. Part of me felt like I was helping Daddy in some way. In his day, deaf children didn't go to school with children who could hear. Now things were different. I could make a difference in the lives of these children.

Everything was going well for me. I had a real job, was earning a decent salary, and I didn't have any school loans to pay back because of the scholarships I received. Daddy's loan that he acquired for me was since paid off, and I was able to earn enough to help Daddy pay some of his bills. It was at this time I became a pledge again in Dover's graduate chapter of Epsilon Iota Omega and finally became an AKA in 1977! Our line was named the Octastyles as there were eight of us. Again, music was

Howard, me, Tawanda, and Karelle.

an important marker of this milestone. I sang "You'll Never Walk Alone" in a final program marking my acceptance into the sorority at the age of twenty-four.

At twenty-five years old, while still working and living with Daddy in Dover, I had rejoined the gospel choir at Whatcoat church. It wasn't the same gospel choir from my teenage years or the gospel choir that I sang with while attending Delaware State. By then, I had also become engaged to Howard and was in the middle of planning our wedding.

One weekend when Howard came back to visit, he said to me, "Let's go out to eat tonight." Of course I was up for that! Any time I didn't have to cook was a treat. While we were seated in one of the booths, Howard pulled out a velvet box, opened it, and put a ring on my finger. He never got down on one knee, or really asked me. After all this time, it was just assumed we'd get married when he had completed his education.

I was singing! The negative voices in my head were retreating. As always, things eventually turned out fine. Life was great!

And as usual in my life when things were going well, I got knocked flat.

Howard had finished his master's and doctorate in experimental psychology at Princeton University in 1978 and was at the beginning of his program for a second doctorate, a PsyD in psychology at Rutgers University. He was actually between degrees because he had not yet participated in the upcoming graduation ceremony at Princeton. He lived in a basement apartment in New Brunswick, NJ, and had a pretty decent social life. His eating habits weren't the healthiest, however.

One night he had attended a party drinking imported cognac with a number of respected doctoral level people at Rutgers. Later, after leaving the party and arriving home at his apartment, he didn't feel like his usual self. He decided to go straight to bed. Honestly, he'd thought it was a hangover. The next morning he awakened and just went on about his day. Not feeling much better, though, he went to a doughnut shop to purchase what turned out to be some pretty salty soup. During the evening hours when he couldn't deny the feeling any longer, he knocked on his upstairs neighbor's apartment and asked them to take him to the hospital. He had to have been feeling extremely bad to ask to go to the hospital, as men try to avoid that trip at all cost and Howard had never in his life needed to go to a hospital.

On his way there, he had blessed the backseat of his neighbor's car with whatever it was that he had eaten just before. By the time he got to the hospital, all he had the energy to do was sign his name. After that he fell into a coma.

While Howard was fighting for his life, on this chilly, but mild April night, the church gospel choir had just returned home to Dover from New Jersey around 11 p.m. from an over two-hour bus trip. The night I got home from the church bus trip, I found a note under the wiper blades of my Aspen that was parked in the church's parking lot. It was a simple note, really. When I think about all the life-changing events, none of them seems as simple as this note that said, "Call Howard's grandmother when you get home."

I shrugged it off. Okay, I'll call Howard's grandmother. I didn't see it as an unusual request. It was April 9, 1978. We were in the throes of planning a huge elaborate wedding, which was only 4 months away almost to the day, August 12, 1978. I had already purchased my dress, and the tuxedos and bridesmaid dresses had been selected and ordered. We had been formally planning our wedding for about a year and were on target with everything that *Bride's Magazine* suggested. His grandmother probably wanted to discuss some minor detail, I thought. I went home, changed into my PJs, got into bed, picked up the phone that was on my nightstand next to my bed, and called her. In a quivering voice she said, "Howard's in the hospital. I don't think he's going to make it."

There was no moment of silence while I digested the information. There was no trying to gather my wits about me. I just let out the longest, most blood curdling scream. Just moments ago things had been fabulous. I was the bride-to-be with a great job, a great fiancé, and a bright future. Now I was facing the prospect of life without Howard. I didn't really see what my other options were at that moment but to scream. That scream contained all the fear in the world for me.

Our most beloved pastor, Rev. Clayton Hammond, was the one who had put the note on my car. He was the one who was going to marry us at Whatcoat United Methodist Church. We felt blessed to have him in our lives. He had driven over to Howard's grandmother's house and was there when I got the news over the phone. I told them both that I was going to drive back to New Jersey that night to see about Howard. Reverend Hammond thought he could talk me out of it, and when he realized I was not going to change my mind, he offered to drive me.

Reverend Hammond turned out to be not only our pastor but one of our greatest friends.

I quickly changed my clothes and woke my dad to tell him the news. Rev. Hammond showed up at my door a few minutes later with Howard's grandmother in the car with him. By this time, my dad had also put on his clothes and declared he was also going. Daddy loved Howard and always said, "Hall, good man." So, it's no wonder that he felt the need to make this trip too.

We all piled into Rev. Hammond's car without one packed bag between us and made the long drive to New Jersey into the wee hours of the morning. On the drive up I could hear Rev. Hammond's stomach growling.

"Are you hungry Rev. Hammond? I feel so bad that you haven't had anything to eat in a while," I said.

"Aw, that's alright I don't get to eat much anyway. I'm trying to stay slim," he would answer.

When we got to St. Peter's Hospital in New Brunswick, New Jersey, the doctors didn't hold out much hope for Howard. One doctor in particular who spoke with us initially seemed to me to be cold and unfeeling. To them, Howard was probably just another young Black man in a coma who they thought had overdosed on some drug. The information was slow in coming and when it did, it was often delivered with a dose of harsh reality.

Finally, it was a young slender African American doctor, an angel really, by the name of Dr. Jothan Staley who told us that Howard had a stroke from a brain aneurism. He was only twenty-eight years old! His doctors gave him a one out of a hundred chance at survival. The cerebral hemorrhage was in a place in Howard's brain that was difficult to access. Dr. Staley felt that the best thing to do was to allow nature to take its course and hope that the rupture would repair itself. The odds were definitely not good. All we could do was pray.

My boss at the Margaret Sterck School was so kind during this time. She allowed me do whatever I needed to do to be there for Howard. For my part, I refused to leave the hospital. Howard's mother Dorothy and father Howard Jr., flew in from Cincinnati later that day. We all stayed together at the hospital. The next day, Rev. Hammond left everyone at the hospital except my dad, who rode back with him to Dover. Howard's

father, a dentist, realized with his medical background the grim progno-
sis, also flew back to Cincinnati the next day as he was having a difficult
time dealing with the idea.

Once Howard stabilized somewhat, I used his black Olds Cutlass
Supreme to drive the three of us—Howard's mother, grandmother, and
me—back to Dover to get some clean clothes and other essentials. We
then returned to New Jersey that same evening and did a daily commute
to the hospital from the basement apartment thereafter until Howard
was out of the woods, which took a total of about three weeks. Family
members would relay messages to my dad that things were progressing.

When Howard came to, his left side was paralyzed. He couldn't walk
or see out of his right eye, and he had suffered short-term memory loss.
Every time I would leave his hospital room to either get something to eat
or visit the ladies room, Howard, upon my return, would become excited
and act as if he were seeing me for the very first time. "Jeanie, Jeanie,
Jeanie," he would chant every time. I got to the point where I would step
outside his room and come back in again just to see his response. It was
like playing peek-a-boo with a grown man. A girl's gotta have a little fun.

Every day at Saint Peter's Hospital, a nurse would shine a flashlight
into Howard's eyes and ask him the standard mental status exam: "Do
you know who you are? Do you know what day it is? Do you know
where you are?" Of course, Howard knew who he was, but had no idea
what day it was or where he was, so the nurse would give him the answers. Eventually, Howard came around and was ready to have some
fun with the nurses. After Howard correctly answered again who he was,
when asked, "Do you know where you are?" Howard just replied "Yes."
After the pause, the nurse asked, "So then, where are you?" Howard
answered, "I am at Saint Peter's Hospital for the criminally insane." She
gave a hearty laugh and responded, "Eventually we may make you that
way." After that, they no longer asked him those questions.

After he recovered and we all realized he'd miraculously beaten the
odds, Fred Gaines, Juanita's husband, drove them both from Cincinnati
to New Jersey so that Juanita could see for herself that her brother was
truly okay. Howard's three vigilant ladies finally were able to leave New
Jersey to go back to Dover. His mother flew back to Cincinnati, and I
went back to work. I'd drive up from Delaware two times a week, once
on Wednesdays late in the afternoon after work, and then back to Dover

late that night in order to get to work on Thursday morning and then drove back to the hospital again on Fridays and stayed until Sunday.

We opted not to change the wedding date. Some people thought we were going to have to push it back a year, but Howard believed he would be ready by August 12th and I believed in Howard just as he had believed in me.

It was going to take nothing less than another miracle to have Howard ready to be able to stand at his own wedding, but I was getting used to the little miracles that kept weaving into our lives. I didn't doubt for a minute that if it was going to take a miracle, then a miracle was what we'd have.

First, however, before the wedding, there was a graduation to attend. Howard's father wheeled Howard in his wheelchair down the streets of Princeton University and to the outdoor area where the ceremony was to take place. Momma Hall, Grandma Johns, Lillian, Juanita, my Daddy, and I walked alongside. Earlier, we all took part in helping Howard don his graduation regalia. That morning it had drizzled a little, but the weather had cleared by the time the ceremony was to begin. Tradition held that it never rains on a Princeton graduation! We were not only proud of Howard's accomplishment, but we were also celebrating his life. Howard was alert and was able to take in all the orange and black sights and sounds of his special day. It was the day he would become Dr. Howard Ralph Hall, III.

When St. Peter's Hospital had done all they could for Howard, he was transferred to Robert Woods Johnson Hospital in Edison, Ohio, for rehabilitation. I made that over two-hour (one way) drive to visit him twice every week for a couple of months without fail. There, Howard worked hard to get back to full strength. There was so much going on in our lives . . . He made magnificent strides to the point that much later in his recovery when the rehab center arranged outings for the residents to attend as a group, Howard was routinely stopped because they couldn't figure out what he was doing hanging out with patients who were obviously more impaired. At these outings, he did use a cane, not because he needed it any longer to walk, but because he thought it was cool having one. He was finally ready to stand unimpeded at our wedding and watch me walk down the aisle.

Expect the Unexpected

YVONNE ELLIMAN SANG MY ANTHEM, "IF I CAN'T HAVE You," and I was planning my wedding. We sent out 500 invitations and got 500+ positive responses. We nicknamed the wedding planner "Dragon Lady." In the true vein of wedding planners, she was going to have a wedding that went off like *she'd* planned it if it meant she had to hog-tie me and Howard to the altar the night before. She didn't seem to get that this day was much bigger than her desire to start exactly on time.

And Howard had done it! He had worked himself to the bone in rehab and physical therapy (or as Howard called it, pain and torture/physical terror) for 4 months, but he had done it. He'd promised that he was going to be walking down the aisle on his own and not with a walker or his cane and without the black patch over his eye that made him look like a pirate. He was going to do it. He'd made a full recovery from his stroke and could stand on his own at our wedding. Nobody thought he could do it. Nobody thought he would do it.

We got married in a standing room only crowd at Whatcoat. Friends, family, doctors, and well-wishers all wanted to see the most recent miracle of our lives. It was not only a wedding, it was another celebration of life. Our guest list was like a who's who among medical professionals and philosopher thinkers. Dr. Cornel West, one of the leading philosophic minds of our time, served as a groomsman as he and Howard had graduated from Princeton together. People were standing in the balcony and lined along the stairs overlooking the main area of the church.

Every bride thinks her wedding was beautiful and I am no different. With the distance of years, I still see that day as one of the most dramatic moments of my life. In all my childhood days, I had never dreamed of a day like the one I had for my candlelight ceremony. Beverly was my maid of honor, Lynne was my junior bridesmaid, and Wilma, a coworker named

Hope and Howard's sisters Lillian and Juanita were my bridesmaids. They were so gorgeous in their long soft yellow dresses. My understanding and outstanding boss served as interpreter and wore a dress that matched the bridesmaids. The flowers they carried surrounded a white candle encased in a hurricane lantern. The flowers were bright, full yellow and had white daisies with baby's breath mixed in with the greenery. The colors were vibrant and awake. My bouquet was full of yellow roses with white baby's breath. Howard's boutonniere was comprised of a single yellow rose with baby's breath and greenery. He wore a handsome all white tuxedo and white shoes to match my stunning white dress that had long sleeves, lace on the bodice, and a long train.

The best man, Phillip Reid, was Howard's childhood friend from Cincinnati. Groomsman Lawrence (Lonnie) Hawkins, Jr., was Lillian's husband and Howard's brother-in-law. Groomsmen Marty Cheatle, Greg McQuater, Larry Morse, and Dr. Cornel West were all Howard's class-mates at Princeton. They and Daddy wore yellow tuxedos with white shirts and white shoes. Their boutonnieres were made from white carna-tions with greenery.

Our flower girl Marty Simms wore a pretty yellow print dress with orange trim. She was the daughter of Carrie Mae and her new husband after Carrie Mae and my cousin Charles became divorced. Our ring bearer, Lawrence, was the three-year-old son of Lonnie and Lillian. He also wore a full white tuxedo.

The song "Evergreen" was melodiously sung by Mrs. Marva Thomas. God was in the church blessing our day, like he had blessed our lives. This day too began with a drizzle, but by the time the wedding started the sky cleared.

Still, as wedding planning goes, it's impossible to plan for everything. The theme of my life had been constant. When I thought things were going well, it then became time for a reality check. We had the major stuff. Howard was there and so was I. But I had changed purses the night before the wedding and had left Howard's ring in my other purse. I didn't realize it until I'd gotten to the church. I had to send Uncle Pick back for my purse and the ring. Meanwhile the wedding planner had her first fit of hysteria for the evening. She didn't want the ceremony to begin late. We were supposed to begin at 4 p.m. sharp! Well, we didn't want to be late either, but I needed the ring! In the meantime, Dragon Lady started the ceremony with the song selections. Luckily, Uncle Pick was able to make it back just as it was time for the bridesmaids to begin their walk.

By then, though, Dragon Lady scared our ring bearer and nephew, Lawrence Hawkins, III, so badly he flat out refused to walk down the aisle. Howard's mother had to walk down with him. Marty Simms, our flower girl, was a little older so I suspect she wasn't as fazed by all the drama.

After our nuptials, Rev. Hammond pronounced us husband and wife. We exited the building to enter our chariot, a pastel yellow Cadillac.

After the wedding, I later found out that Howard's brother-in-law, Lonnie, a larger guy, had a tuxedo that didn't fit so he had to go to Philadelphia the morning of the wedding to find a yellow tuxedo that fit. Then he found out that the shoes were too small. He did manage to wear them for the duration of the ceremony, consciously ignoring the pain. Luckily, it all worked out.

And then there was the Nick issue. It didn't really qualify as true wedding crasher potential, but it was still one more dramatic moment in what was quickly turning into a sea of drama.

Nick was a child I had worked with when I was in high school. One of the summer jobs I held was as a tutor of sorts for the migrant children that seasonally came to Dover to work in the agricultural fields. The migrant summer school program was provided by Dover's educational system. Nick and I formed a close friendship, so I sent him and his family an announcement of my wedding. They were migrant workers who lived in Florida in the off-season and they had not RSVP'd. The last thing I expected was a phone call from them the night before the wedding saying they were at the Philadelphia airport and needed a ride into Dover. But that's what I got. In hindsight, I don't know why I didn't expect it. With the way things were going, it should not have surprised me.

My groomsmen offered to go and get Nick and his mother, but I was concerned for their safety as we had just concluded the rehearsal dinner, complete with alcoholic beverages. A two-hour ride to the Philadelphia airport late at night was a huge concern for me. I wanted to be sure they were at my wedding in good shape. So I called the airport and had them make an announcement over the intercom to get Nick and his mother to come to the phone. Amazingly enough they heard the message and came to the phone. I felt so badly that I had to tell them that I didn't have anyone who could come to pick them up and could they find a ride down to Dover. They actually managed to find someone to drive them and showed up at my front door early in the morning the day of my wedding. I had them stay at my house since Howard and I had reservations for that evening at the Sheraton Hotel where the reception was being held. Nick's mother slept in my bedroom and Nick slept on the living room sofa. Daddy was not pleased. Howard and I had a relatively early flight the next morning out of Philadelphia to go to Jamaica to start our honeymoon, so we wanted to be able to leave Dover in enough time to make the international flight.

At the reception, Nick approached me and asked if he and his mother could catch a ride to the airport with Howard and me the next day. Again, I was feeling awful about this whole scene. This was not the image I had dancing around in my head as newlyweds embarking on our new lives together. I was also worried that something would go wrong and we would miss our flight. What if they weren't ready to go when it came time? I didn't want to seem rude. I spoke to Howard about this situation and he said he didn't mind playing the heavy. He, with much grace, explained that we just could not do it. I hated spending my wedding evening on such a negative note, worrying about hurting their feelings, but I would have felt much worse had Howard not intervened.

I think possibly Nick's mother had a crush on Daddy, which may have been what prompted the impromptu appearance at my wedding. But, Daddy did not reciprocate these feelings and let me know it.

We took over three full banquet rooms at the Dover Sheraton for the reception. The event planner at the hotel had tried to talk me out of that. "Nobody," she'd said, "has ever had a wedding that large." She'd said it in a way that made me know that Howard and I weren't expected to fill a room that large if "nobody" else had been able to do it. The "nobody" in this case being the "all-important" folks of Dover with money and connections. I can still see her incredulous expression as the guests filed in one behind the other in a never-ending line, filling up the public space and altering her consciousness at the same time. She had no way of knowing that she was in the room with some of America's most relevant critical thinkers on just about everything.

The thing you learn when you're planning a wedding is not to expect it to run smoothly. If you expect the unexpected then nothing surprises you and by default everything runs smoothly. It all turned out to be a wonderful celebration.

Paradise

OUR HONEYMOON IN JAMAICA WAS THE FINAL TEST OF Howard's fitness. I could hardly wait to get started. I had seen the commercials and read the brochures cover to cover at least ten times.

Our plane landed at Montego Bay and Howard and I disembarked, ready to see the world. All the expectation of Jamaica was written on our expressions. We were struck immediately by the overwhelming contrast. The island was beautiful. That word doesn't quite seem enough. Breathtaking! The scenery was awesome, in the truest definition of the word. It was impossible to look out over the blooming flowers and dynamic colors in Nature's palette and not see a divine presence. For a minute I thought we had stumbled *into* the brochures I'd been poring over for the last few months. Hibiscus was in bloom everywhere in color combinations I had never imagined. Red and blue and purple and yellow exploded in the space around us. The land was aquiver with plant life. Where there wasn't tropical flora it was remarkably green and not the kind of green that I was used to. It was a deep dark, lush green, carpets of it. Few of us could resist the temptation to reach out and touch some of the greenery to be certain we weren't being deceived by plastic. By contrast, it made the grass I remembered from home seem positively lifeless.

What I didn't want was the real world intruding on my paradise. It wasn't fair as far as I was concerned. The brochures didn't say anything about the real world. They didn't mention abject poverty and capitalist consumers and producers. The brochures hadn't warned us about this new wrinkle and it took us a minute to wrap our collective thoughts around the idea that this was the place we had chosen to begin our lives. I swallowed my guilt as we rode through the opulent countryside to our hotel and bore witness to the markings of capitalism.

We were headed to Falmouth, Jamaica, to stay at the Trelawney Beach Hotel between Ocho Rios and Montego Bay. It was like entering another world. In the interior of the country was the poverty and human neglect, but on the outskirts was paradise. I think I should have felt even guiltier than I did. But I was able to leave the reality of daily Jamaica life behind me the further out we got. By the time we reached our hotel, I had been transported, mind and body.

Pristine. Someone understood how to pamper a tourist. The resort was wide open, clean and crisp from the décor to the service. Seamless hospitality. It was like we had entered our very own palace.

Our living quarters was one of the few grass hut cottages at the back of the hotel that followed a winding path, peppered with palm trees and flowers, to the beach. I had never been so enchanted. The huts were set in what I was beginning to see was a trademark garden setting. Every morning we were awakened with the smells of breakfast of various pastries and tea with milk. I don't know what it was about the tea, but it was the best tea I'd ever tasted. Maybe it was the milk. Maybe it was the honeymoon. I didn't know, but I had to try and find out. I asked the waiter to find out what kind of tea it was. I couldn't get enough of it. Well, the next day he came back with the box and showed me that it was plain old Lipton tea! I still don't know what they did to it over there but I can't duplicate the taste even today. It must have been the water.

In the afternoon we spent our time horseback riding, shopping, and bartering in Ocho Rios. That was an adventure. We were still working off the guilt that the poverty of the interior induced in us and the concept of bargaining seemed somehow unseemly. Once we came to understand that they expected us to barter, Howard had no problem pretending he didn't want something that we wanted very badly. Howard was a whiz at the bartering process. "Ten dollar, ten dollar," the merchant would say in that beautiful Jamaican accent. Howard would turn the item over and over in his hands just the way my dad would do with a pair of popular shoes that I wanted him to purchase for me. At the end of his inspection always came, "no good" as he tossed the shoe back. Howard would assert to the merchant "five dollars," to which the merchant would come back with "eight" and so on until they both reached a happy compromise.

While we were in Jamaica, I assumed we were going to see Dunn's River Falls, a popular tourist attraction. It's funny when I look back on it, but at the time, not so much. Howard was technically still recovering. He was still partially blind in one eye and not quite sure on his feet. I think it was the ocean air and hibiscus flowers that must have gone to our heads. We got caught up, as they say. But anyway, we had planned this outing and we were going to do it. According to the brochure, you couldn't come to that part of Jamaica and not do the falls. What else could we do?

Mind you, Dunn's River Falls is a 600-foot rise of rock and water. It's really quite a charming activity if you're fit and ready for a workout. To climb it, the guide has everyone link hands and climb in a kind of chain-link fashion. That should have been our first clue. But Howard and I, like many of the people on this adventure, were newlyweds and our heads were still full of the adventure of being married and the thrill of being amidst such exquisite beauty. About halfway up we figured out that this wasn't going to work for a man just getting over a stroke.

Howard had begun to get dizzy and his footing got a little loose. Well, we hadn't come this far to lose him to a 600-foot rise of rock, so we decided to get off at the next available spot. Fortunately, about halfway up there was a wonderful place to exit and watch everyone else finish the climb. It would have been fun to go to the top, but to say I regret not going the full height would be wrong. It didn't matter from what angle you viewed the raw countryside of Jamaica, it was all majestic.

We also learned a song while we were relaxing on the beach. We learned it from a Rastafarian. He was an older gentleman who sat on the beach singing and attracting attention. The song was about the rampant capitalist exploitation of the native population. Again, I was confronted with my guilt at having to claim part of that responsibility. The song didn't help.

Concrete Castle King
Won't you give us a helping hand
Concrete Castle King
Can't you see that we're sufferin'

Livin' in a two by four
With no place to walk around
While you're in a castle all alone.

There's more to it than that, but you get the gist. I know I certainly did.

Still, it was a beautiful honeymoon in a beautiful country. Howard and I began our charmed life as a married couple in one of the most exquisite places on earth. *Yeah mon!*

Back at the resort, Howard and I participated in the talent show and everyone raved about our performance. Howard played and I sang Phyllis Hyman's version of the 1972 classic by the Stylistics, "Betcha By Golly Wow," written by Thom Bell and Linda Creed. A lot of the people there thought Howard was a professional musician and I was a professional singer from the United States. And we won!

The Real World

FOR ALL THE BEAUTY OF JAMAICA, I WAS GLAD TO BE BACK home. I was ready to start our real life together and get down to the business of making a life. Howard's time was spent working on his second doctorate in psychology at Rutgers University. By this time, he had graduated wearing his colors of black and orange from Princeton and was now focused on obtaining a new color—scarlet. I, on the other hand, dove into my chosen profession.

I was able to obtain work with the New Jersey Commission for the Blind working as an itinerant teacher primarily in the southern half of New Jersey, providing services to children who were both deaf and blind. It was kind of the same job I had in Delaware at the Sterck School. I visited and worked with the children at their various schools. The only difference was that I was expected to conduct home visits in this new position. The teachers often didn't have any idea what to do with these children. Students who were deaf and blind needed a different kind of instruction than students who could see and hear. I brought to the teachers ideas and materials, gave them support, and helped them understand how to reach children who couldn't be reached using traditional methods. I also visited the families of these children in their homes to make sure their needs were being met there as well.

It was a hard job, but I was having a ball. While Howard was chipping away at his new studies, I was up and down the New Jersey Turnpike and the Garden State Parkway. I never had trouble making friends. And I made a lot of "friends" along the highway because I stopped at every mall I could see. (I stopped so frequently, at one point, employees there thought I worked at the mall too.)

But it was a great job. I was young and unencumbered. I saw no reason why I shouldn't enjoy myself.

I even made friends at the toll booths on the parkway and the turn-pike. I drove it every day. It would have been downright rude to drive past someone every day and never smile or say hello. After a while I just got to know people. It has to be hard enough working those booths every day, trying not to succumb to the monotony of the task without having to stare at blank faces in the process. So I smiled, a lot.

After a while, people got to know me and I got to know them. We had a special bond with the highway. It can be a lonely place, for the traveler and the ticket taker. For me, I was often in the car alone with the radio. Sure, I had company when I reached my destination, but there was a lot of road between destinations sometimes. It was nice to be able to smile and say hello to a friendly familiar face.

The world is far too short on friendly familiar faces as it is. If everyone understood how far a smile or a friendly greeting can actually go, I sus-pect everyone would do it on a regular basis. Most people are content to live their lives on the periphery, barely being noticed and barely noticing anything. They're just getting by. I never wanted to live my life like that, not then and certainly not now.

By this point, Howard and I had been together for a while now and were coming upon an important milestone. There is a tradition in many families where the top tier of the wedding cake is saved to eat on the first anniversary. Well, my dad didn't know about this tradition. When Howard and I went back to Dover to retrieve our cake and eat it on the anniversary of our first year together, clumps of it had been cut and con-sumed. My dad thought there was no reason to let a perfectly good piece of cake go uneaten for a year. I was mortified!

Another Test

WE LIVED IN OLD BRIDGE, NEW JERSEY, FOR TWO YEARS. When Howard finished up his education at Rutgers in 1980 and could now add red and white to his collection of regalia colors, we moved to State College, Pennsylvania. Howard got his first job at Penn State University, home of the Nittany Lions, the colors of blue and white. Howard was on the faculty in the Psychology Department and I was able to land a position as an instructor in the Department of Communication Disorders. As luck would have it, we worked in the same building. I was on the first floor of the Moore Building while Howard was on the third.

In this job, I taught courses in ASL, Deaf culture, and in education of the Deaf, and supervised student teachers around the state. Once again I was doing a lot of driving. It was during this time I discovered I had an ovarian cyst.

The symptoms did not come on suddenly. I had lived with the pain for years before I decided to do anything about it. My menstrual cycles were excruciatingly painful. When I bent over, I could feel the lump in my pelvic area. I finally went to see a doctor when the lump began to affect my walking.

We had no children at the time and the doctors were saying I might have to sacrifice my fallopian tubes. At that point, they were not sure if both tubes had been affected. I cannot describe the fear and dread that accompanied that information. In addition to the fear of cancer, I had to face the unavoidable and real possibility that I might never have children of my own.

The cyst required surgery and I bet I counted every second on the clock until I could get some resolution. I checked into the local State College hospital with my heart in my throat. My faith and experience had taught me that God would see me through this. My relationship with

Howard and the ordeal we had gone through made it possible for me to rely more heavily on my faith. I knew he would be there, as a constant in my life. I would never have been able to get through the fear and anxiety if it had not been for those two stable forces in my life.

I admit I asked the typical questions, despite my faith. *Why me?* I was young, hadn't lived my life yet. I hadn't lived perfectly, but I hadn't done anyone any intentional harm. I tried to do unto others as I would have them do unto me. All of that entered into my conversations with the Creator during this time.

At the hospital, Pappa Hall had called me to reassure me that all would be well. Howard's dad had always made me feel that I was another one of his daughters and his acceptance of me meant everything. It made his call that much more special. When it was time for my surgery, I sent up one last prayer, kissed Howard and told him I loved him, and let them put me to sleep.

When I awoke, the doctor told me that my cyst was as large as a grapefruit, but was benign, my fallopian tubes were intact, and that I would be able to have children. It felt like I had shed a ton of bricks. I believe that I have a strong faith, but at times everyone's strength is tested. I don't know what I would have done if the doctor had told me that the cyst was malignant and that I would have to sacrifice my fallopian tubes. I don't even like to think about it. But when I do think about it, I like to think that I would have continued to rely on my faith to get me through. After all the worry and all the tears, Howard and I would be able to go back to our lives and think about planning for additions to our family. Hallelujah!

Our Bundle of Joy

IN JUNE OF 1982, AT TWENTY-NINE YEARS OF AGE, I BECAME pregnant with my first daughter Ilea, while Howard and I were teaching at Penn State. In addition to his regular teaching assignment, Howard, now thirty-two, also worked with the Penn State Athletic Department as the team psychologist, specifically with the football team and Joe Paterno. For a term, Howard was vice president and I was treasurer of the Forum on Black Affairs, a Black faculty/staff group that provided a platform for any issues that affected us and Black students. Howard was debating the usefulness of standardized tests to determine athletic eligibility. Joe Paterno was the guest speaker of our meeting that late March evening, and I was nearing my due date. And I was tired.

Thank goodness for my friend. She was a Deaf woman who also taught at Penn State. She was married to a hearing professor. Together they had a beautiful daughter who reminded me so much of myself as a young Coda. I remember when she was born and how quickly she learned to sign and interpret for her mother. My friend was gracious enough to lend me all of her maternity clothes so that I could look professional without having to go into debt buying a whole new maternity wardrobe.

The night of Joe's presentation, I was wearing one of her outfits and would have gladly stretched out on the floor and given birth right then and there if things had worked out that way. Being a mom was the most exciting thing that had happened to me since my marriage. I was giddy with anticipation. But the baby wasn't really showing the same anticipation at seeing me. At that point I thought I was going to be pregnant forever. Joe Paterno saved me from that fate. He approached me with a big smile after the forum meeting was over and asked me about my due date. I told him I was ready, but the baby wasn't really feeling this birthing thing. He smiled again and asked if he might move things along with his

Paterno Twist. At this point in the process I didn't think I had anything to lose. So I gave my permission and he put his hands on my arms and gave my body a light twisting motion that went back and forth. He said, "You'll be having that baby in the next twenty-four hours."

"Okay, yeah right," I said doubtingly.

At home that night Howard was up late preparing his lecture for the next day when I felt my first labor pains. "Howard," I said, trying not to create a panic either in myself or him. "Howard, I think you need to come to bed and get some rest. I'm feeling something."

Howard was knee deep into planning his lecture. I'm not even sure he heard me. If he did I'm not sure he believed me. In any case, I think he thought if he ignored me, the pain I was having would go away until the timing was more convenient for him. Finally, he yelled back from the office, "Just get some rest and we will have the baby in the morning." I persisted until he finally came into our bedroom and told me he was going to call the doctor. It was 3 a.m. He was sure the doctor would reassure me that it was nothing. Much to Howard's surprise, the doctor told him to get me to the hospital immediately!

Ilea Elizabeth Mosley Hall was born three hours later. She cried—a lot. Ilea was such a beautiful baby with lots of dark hair and a slight slant in her eyes like Howard and his sister Lillian, and very light in complexion. Howard and I were so delighted to have our first child. Howard's complexion was a bit darker so when he dressed to go into the nursery to see his first born, the nurses promptly told him that the area is for fathers only, to which he promptly replied, "I am a father!"

When it was time to take Ilea home, the nurses kept checking to make sure they were giving us the correct baby. They checked her wristband with mine, left the room, and then came back again for another check, making absolutely sure she was ours. I can't blame them as Ilea had more of an Asian look that the staff didn't know how to deal with. Joe Paterno called the hospital the day Ilea was born and said, "See, I told you the Paterno Twist works!" I laughed and gave him his props. We brought our little bundle of joy home and enjoyed being first-time parents.

In recent times, Joe received a bad rap for the Sandusky incident that appeared all over the news media. Some people felt he should have done more to bring the unfortunate occurrence to light. If you knew him, you would know that he was always on the side of his students' best interest. He was a moral and upright man who unfortunately got caught up in hindsight being 20/20. Howard, having worked with Joe and members of the Penn State football team, said Joe had a reputation of stating emphatically that while the team was on the road, if he ever caught any of his coaches fooling around, he would fire them on the spot and they would have to find their own way back home. I'm sure that we have all faced times when in the moment we did not respond the way we would have if we had the benefit of hindsight. I'm so glad that in recent times Joe was given back his college football wins and reputation. No doubt all of the stress caused by the negative publicity was instrumental in his passing.

Jamaica Again, Really!

WHILE WE WERE IN STATE COLLEGE, HOWARD AND I looked for interesting ways to amuse ourselves, in addition to taking care of our one-year-old. It was 1984 when one day, listening to the radio, we heard that the station was conducting a contest. They were soliciting entries for a Pepsi jingle. The writer of the best jingle would win a free trip to Jamaica. Guess where in Jamaica?! Yep. The same place we went for our honeymoon.

I loved Jamaica and I loved music. The contest was tailor-made for us. So Howard wrote the lyrics and tune and we made a cassette tape with me singing the jingle. In no time, we had a catchy tune we thought could be the winning entry.

I walked it down to the radio station with Ilea in tow and handed it to the station manager and said, "Here's your winning tape." Of course he laughed. We both did.

Days later, he called and told me that it had indeed been the winning jingle. He told me that the radio station would be calling me at 3 o'clock and that I was to act excited, like I was hearing the news for the first time. No problem. I was also a great actress. Years later, once we moved to Cleveland, we made a video for Diet Pepsi for another contest using the same song, but with a few upgrades. We weren't as fortunate in that one, but it was fun to make using the luscious and enchanting Cleveland Greenhouse as a backdrop.

Howard, Ilea, and I returned to the exact same resort where we'd honeymooned 6 years earlier. It was just as much fun the second time around. Since we could only bring two bags each, I decided that we could pack more if I took cloth diapers for Ilea instead of using up our bag allotment with disposables.

Bad idea.

When we again arrived at the Trelawney Beach Hotel, we unpacked our bags and began our lovely vacation. Once there, it seemed that Ilea was going through her diapers much more quickly than usual. I was hand washing them, but they were not drying fast enough. I was starting to panic. What would I do if the diapers ran out? We had 6 more days to go!

The concierge was kind enough to explain the situation to another American couple with a baby about the same age staying at the hotel and asked if they wouldn't mind sharing some of their disposable diapers with me. I'm sure that mother had counted out the number she thought she could get by with, but she was the guardian angel that I needed. She said yes. She gave me enough diapers to get by on until the concierge was able to, on her day off, drive to the closest town (which was about an hour away) that had a store that actually carried disposable diapers. They were not that prevalent in Jamaica as they were in the United States.

She returned with a big smile and a huge bag of disposable diapers, the equivalent of gold. We hugged. After our vacation was over and we returned to the states, the concierge and I kept in touch for several years. We have since been out of touch, but I thank her for her kindness and friendship. I offered the mother who so generously shared with me replacements, but they were not needed. I thanked them both profusely then, and I'm thanking them again now!

Mr. Mandela

ALSO IN 1984, I RECALLED HEARING A RIVETING SONG ON the radio that would later become known as the anthem for the protest movement in South Africa: "Free Nelson Mandela." At the time, I had no clue as to who this person was, but he must have been important to have so many Whites and Blacks talking about him and for people to be writing songs to advocate for his release from prison. Howard and I began to pay attention to any news that would enlighten us more about this man. Gil Scott-Heron had penned a song about what was going on in Johannesburg. Pictures appeared on the TV screen of the Archbishop Desmond Tutu and Mr. Mandela's wife, Winnie, marching arm in arm, demanding the release of Mr. Mandela.

A new word that I had not heard before had been used to describe this protest: Apartheid, meaning *apartness*. Famous Americans such as singer, actor, and activist Harry Belafonte, actor and activist Sidney Poitier, and tennis great Arthur Ash were doing their part to shed light on this atrocity and working diligently to get the message out to us in the United States about what was going on.

Songs that were played on the radio about the horrors of Apartheid really helped us as unknowing Americans make a connection to our brothers and sisters in a foreign land. It encouraged us to do what we could to support them. The most I could ever do was be informed, but that was better than ignorance. I felt a need deep within me to do something, but what? South Africa was a million miles away. I heard via the news on TV that those involved in making a difference were calling for the Reagan administration to do something about supporting the idea that American companies should divest from South Africa and for Americans to boycott those businesses that were in support of the old South African regime that favored Apartheid.

My contribution to the cause was to participate in the boycott. That was something I could do. I made sure that I did not purchase any items from any of the businesses on the list. I guess my early exposure to the political scene from Daddy was still part of my political consciousness.

Thanks to a recent interview conducted by news personality Roland Martin on the Tom Joyner Morning Show, a syndicated radio program focused on African American music and culture, it was brought to our attention that the whole divestment movement was actually started by an African American group of Polaroid workers led by Caroline Hunter. They were known as the Polaroid Workers Revolutionary Movement. Polaroid had been in South Africa since 1937. They made the passbooks the South African government required Blacks to carry on their person at all times. If they were caught without it, they could be arrested. These passbooks had a photo ID and information that could prove you were a citizen. Once the Polaroid workers found out about the underground involvement of their company in Apartheid, they launched a protest that began the divestment movement. Carolyn Hunter was fired from Polaroid for her participation in the boycott. She eventually became an educator and seems to be no worse for the wear. More about this story can be found on www.blackamericaweb.com.

Finally, Mr. Mandela's release was obtained in 1990, but he had already been incarcerated for twenty-seven years! Images of the protest of the segregated system of Apartheid reminded me of the scenes I had recalled from the days people had marched in this country with the Rev. Dr. Martin Luther King Jr. TV images showing how Bull Connor had his policemen spraying water from fire hoses on American citizens and allowing police dogs to attack them were appalling. Even though I didn't grow up hearing about the plight of South Africans of color, it was easy for me to identify with this movement because of our Civil Rights movement here at home.

It was eye opening for me to see that people of color in other parts of the world were experiencing the same fate as people of color had in this country. It helped me to see that we were not alone in this fight and the importance of forging a bond to create unity with our brothers and sisters all over the world to convey a unified message of equality for all. I was proud when our nation would come to support the abolishment of South Africa's two-tiered system that gave privileges to the minority ruling Europeans while requiring the majority Blacks to serve.

In 2000, it was like coming full circle when I had several opportunities to meet the daughter of Archbishop Desmond Tutu, once when she was an invited speaker at Penn State, and again when she was working with one of the advisors on my doctoral dissertation from Cleveland State University, Dr. Raymond Winbush.

Dr. Winbush decided to leave Cleveland State after a time and had taken a position of Director for an African American Studies Department at Fisk University in Nashville, Tennessee. Nontombi Tutu was assisting him in this position. We were looking at colleges for our oldest daughter Ilea to attend for her undergraduate studies and Fisk was on the list. Since I had heard Dr. Winbush was there, I contacted him and was able to schedule a tour of the campus with him and Naomi, who bears a very strong resemblance to her father.

Howard, Ilea, our second daughter Karelle, and I took pictures together with Naomi and Dr. Winbush, had lunch together, and heard the valuable history of the campus from which the great Dr. W.E.B. DuBois graduated. Ilea eventually decided to attend and later graduated from Tennessee State University, which is right down the road from Fisk. Howard and I were excited that Ilea had found her niche and that she was happy with her decision. Thank you Naomi and Dr. Winbush for sharing your valuable time with us and for a most enjoyable day!

The Nursing Home Blues

WITH DADDY SPRAWLED OUT ON THE LAWN WAITING FOR the ambulance that Mommom had called, my world would be forever changed. Howard and I had to think. What did we need to do? We made the necessary arrangements with our jobs, and packed up Ilea and our bags for a trip to visit Daddy in the hospital in Dover. He was shaken up. He was also bruised, pretty sore, and had a cracked rib.

While there we tried to think about where he should go upon recovery and make those arrangements. He didn't have the finances to live in one of those fancy nursing homes. Daddy didn't have the kind of insurance that would even cover a regular nursing home stay. As luck would have it, there was one place he could go.

The hospital social worker was the one who gave us the name of a husband and wife who ran a facility out of their home. They took in recuperating hospital patients for the amount of their monthly social security check. When he recovered enough to be transported, he rode in an ambulance to get there. I didn't really want to put him in a nursing home facility, but he couldn't be alone. And I didn't have the resources to take him home to Pennsylvania with me.

Daddy would have loved that. He didn't really want anybody else to take care of him. But I was a newlywed and we were not yet in stable positions. Daddy needed around-the-clock care. There were no facilities in State College that could provide what he needed at a cost we could afford. I was still trying to set up my home. Even to my own ears the reasons sound contrived, hollow, and guilt ridden, but I know that the pain of telling him we were not able to take care of him the way he needed was far less than the pain it would have caused us all to say "yes" to his desire to come live with me and Howard at that time. Besides, he had the rest of his family in Dover to visit and look out for him in between my visits. He would be spending much of his time alone if he were to live with me.

The home was located at the end of a long country dirt road on the outskirts of Dover. It was very difficult to find; no signs, just a turn left at the big pine tree at the fork in the road after you pass the big red barn. There wasn't much to it. They were White, but the patients they helped were all males and mostly, if not all, Black. They kept a clean home. She had a common room where the patients ate and watched television. And she had dogs.

I wasn't able to visit as much as Daddy probably would have liked, but I came down when I could. Mommom kept me posted on how Daddy was doing for the most part. On her visits, she was always good about telling me how nice it was and that Daddy was in good hands.

I thought initially that I had left him in good hands at the nursing home, but sometimes you have nagging doubts that play at the back of your mind. Daddy said things when I came to visit such as he wasn't getting any food or the woman wouldn't feed him. When I came to visit, the woman who took care of him seemed like a nice enough person. She smiled when she was supposed to smile and said the things she was supposed to say.

I thought maybe Daddy was working me, trying to get me to let him come live with me. Still something nagged at me and still does. I would like to think Daddy would have found a way to make me believe if something was truly wrong, but I don't know. Sometimes it tugs at me in the middle of the night, but I know I'll never know the answer to that now. I calm myself with the idea that it is just my guilt playing at the edges of my mind making me think I didn't do the right thing. It's all I have.

When Daddy was settled into the nursing home we went to clean out the house. Someone had broken in once; we didn't need a repeat performance now that the house was empty. It was a difficult process. It felt a little like burglary, even in a house I'd lived in most of my life. Worse than that, it was like an erasure. It's the people who are left behind who have to go in and clean up. It's an ugly compromise. But it had to be done and so we did it.

It was while we were going through drawers that we found the money. Daddy, growing up in the Depression era, still didn't trust banks, and maybe his reasons were more practical than that. He was a Deaf man in a hearing culture. It was probably very difficult for him to trust the care and keeping of his money with strangers. It was $11,000! That's how much cash Daddy had tucked away in an old rumpled brown paper bag. In hindsight, we figured that that's probably what prompted the break-in. How anybody knew is really anyone's guess. Maybe they didn't really know. Maybe they only suspected. Maybe that wasn't it at all.

Thankfully, I was able to tell Daddy that we'd found his money and that it was safe. The relief that washed over his face when I told him was priceless. That at least gave him some peace.

The Call

CALLS LIKE THIS ALWAYS SEEM TO COME IN THE MIDDLE of the night. It was a warm spring late night in May 1984. The lady at the nursing home called. In a very calm and deliberate tone, she said "Hi, Jeanie, your daddy has gone. The dogs started to bark loudly, so loudly and persistently that I had to get up and go to where your daddy sleeps. He wasn't breathing, so I called the ambulance. He's on his way to Kent General Hospital in Dover, now."

I knew the day would eventually come, but you can never be totally ready for it. I cried, not an all-out sobbing, but the tears gently flowed down my cheek, while Howard, who was now alert and by my side, rubbed my back. I thanked her for all she had done for Daddy.

She talked about how funny he was when he would get mad at her because he thought she had too many men. Earlier, I had brought her a sign language book to help her, her husband, and Daddy communicate better. She really did seem genuine.

After, I was able to gain my composure and I went right into business mode. Things had to be done. I did not have time for overt grief. Daddy had been deteriorating for a while. It wasn't like this was a surprise to any of us. Mommom worked for Mr. Howard Stevenson, the undertaker who had been a childhood friend of the family. That helped a lot with the little things. I had never planned a funeral before. Daddy made his transition on Monday, May 14, 1984. He was sixty-nine years old.

Daddy lasted less than a year after the beating. He only got to spend a little time with Ilea. She was just a year old when he died. I took her a few times to see him, but of course she doesn't remember it except for what I've told her. I was so grateful for what little time I did have to bring Ilea and Daddy together on visits we made to the nursing home before he made his transition. It was a bittersweet time for me. I had to make a lot of difficult decisions about my life and life now without my daddy.

He never wanted anybody but me to take care of him and my moving away seemed like a betrayal to him. I fought the impetus to blame myself for leaving him. I worked hard to convince myself of my right to live my life on my own. I had never thought of my father as handicapped, even if he had needed me for things most children didn't have to do for their parents. I looked at what I did for him like what any child of non-English speaking parents would have to do. No more.

Most of the arrangements were made over the phone until we were ready to make another trip to Dover. I went to the old Farmers Bank to withdraw the small amount of Daddy's money he had decided to deposit. Except for what we had found, it was really all the money he had in the world. Funerals were expensive even then. I got to the counter and handed over the withdrawal slip and waited. The teller behind the counter announced that he could not release the money to me. I took a deep breath and tried to explain things to him. He was not hearing it.

I could feel my pulse quicken and my blood pressure rose spontaneously with the level of my ire. What was I going to do now? The bank had a right, I guess, to protect its assets, but what about me? I needed to bury my father and it was his money, after all. I felt the tears start to well in my eyes. My body had ceased its resistance. My shoulders drooped without my consent. I was done and near hysterics.

It was right about that moment a high school classmate of mine who worked at the bank came in from her lunch break and was willing to vouch for me. She told the teller who I was and that it was okay to give me the money. Now I know why Daddy didn't really want to be bothered with banks. What if that woman hadn't been there? Still, I was grateful.

We had a beautiful home going ceremony for Daddy at Whatcoat, even though he had never attended. It was our family's church. We buried Dad at Sharon Hills out near Route 8 in the same area where the rest of the current family had purchased burial plots. My paternal grandparents' generation had been buried at Fork Branch and my paternal great-grandparents are interred at the Indian Mission Church cemetery.

As you will recall, Daddy's shoe shop where he did all his business was right next door to our house. Next to the shoe shop was an empty lot.

After all those years, I still called it the shoe shop because that's what it was first and my memories of my childhood of being in that shop are so precious. However, over the years after Daddy closed the shoe shop, he turned it into a sub shop where my cousin Charles and Dot sold sandwiches. Then Daddy turned it into a small apartment that he rented out. After Daddy's death, I sold the house and the shoe shop to the folks who put a carwash next door. Another sign of the changing times, I guess.

Howard and I tried to keep the house for a while. We rented it out, but it got back to us that there was a lot of curious activity going on around the place. At one point, there were a suspicious number of people all living in that small two-bedroom house. One count had it at thirteen. I don't know if that number included the one they discovered living under the house (we had no basement) and really, I don't care. Thirteen was too many.

The Stork Strikes Again

DURING DADDY'S ORDEAL, HOWARD AND I HAD JUST purchased our first home, a condo on Galen Drive, State College, Pennsylvania. Our second daughter Karelle Ayita Hall was born in 1986, two years after Daddy passed. Karelle was born just before we moved to Cleveland. No Paterno Twist this time, but the same joy. Ilea was three years old and was just getting over a bout of chicken pox that she received at a chicken pox party. This of course, was in the days before there was a vaccine. Parents would find out that a friend's child had the childhood disease and then bring their child over so that their child could be exposed and get it over with before they entered kindergarten.

We had enrolled Ilea in a Big Sister program offered by the local hospital. One of the activities encouraged the big sister to create a sock doll for the new sibling that would then be placed in the new baby's crib at the hospital just after birth. The doll Ilea created for Karelle was very different from the other dolls. This doll had dots painted all over. When we asked Ilea why her doll looked this way, she replied, "It has chicken pox!" We all chuckled and thought it was such a creative gift to her little sister.

With Karelle, I began feeling labor pains very late in the evening just like with Ilea. Thank goodness for our neighbors, Earl and Barbara Merritt, who lived in a condo across the parking lot from ours. Howard and I had previously arranged for them to come and stay with Ilea when it was time for us to go to the hospital to bring Karelle into the world. They graciously got up from their nice warm beds in the wee hours of the morning: 3 a.m. again!

About three hours later, just like Ilea, and a little before 6 a.m., Karelle was born. She remained with me, just as Ilea did, in my hospital room the entire three days I was there, except for when the nurses took her for whatever it was they did in those nurseries. Karelle also had lots of dark hair and beautiful, big, round, dark, shiny eyes like Howard's father, Papa Hall. Papa Hall called them the Coleman eyes.

I remember that Karelle, unlike her sister, really didn't cry much at all and was a very content baby. The one peep I heard from her was when I had to put her down so that I could go to the restroom. It was as if she were calling me: "eh, eh, eh." It was the cutest little sound. As soon as I came back to her, she was content again looking up at me with those beautiful big brown eyes. This time when it was time to take her home, there were no unusual wristband checks and rechecks. We left the hospital with Karelle, excited to show her off to her big sister. Howard and I were now the happy and proud parents of two gorgeous baby girls!

Karelle, like her sister, attended schools in the Shaker Heights School system, graduated, and attended college. Her first choice was to attend Dartmouth. As she opened the letter from them and discovered that she was accepted, Howard and I were elated for her that her dream had come true.

Another Move

IN SEPTEMBER OF 1987, HOWARD WAS OFFERED A POSITION at Rainbow Babies and Children's Hospital in Cleveland, Ohio, to work with Dr. Karen Olness, a famous physician in the area of hypnosis and biofeedback.

There is a funny story about the first time they met. Howard was attending a conference on hypnosis and biofeedback and ran into Dr. Olness in an elevator. He was carrying his briefcase that had a Penn State logo.

She saw the briefcase and said, "Oh, Penn State! Do you know Howard Hall?"

He replied, "I am Howard Hall."

After they chuckled, she stated that she had just accepted a position at University Hospitals CASE Medical Center in Cleveland (now known as Cleveland Medical Center) and would he be interested in joining her there as a member of her team to do research and help her set up a new lab in hypnosis and biofeedback? Well, as luck (or the multiverse) would have it, Howard was on the market as he did not receive tenure from Penn State and had a year to look for a position elsewhere.

When we first learned that we would have to move again, we saw this denial as another wrinkle. We should have known something better was coming.

At the same time, Howard was also looking at Northeastern in Boston as a possible opportunity for employment. I went to Boston with Howard. As usual, I had to find a job too. I had an interview during the same week that Howard would be interviewing at Northeastern. The girls were very young—ages one and four—and I didn't want to leave them behind. So we made a family trip of it. It wasn't like a real vacation being that it was winter in Boston, but we were away from our usual lodgings so we wanted to enjoy the opportunity.

Karelle and Ilea came with me to my interview. That by itself wasn't really the problem. It was after the interview that things got a little sticky. When my interview was over, I needed to get the girls back to the hotel. It was cold, snowy, and wet, and they hadn't eaten in a while. We had flown into Boston, so I needed to get around by cab. I wasn't confident enough that I could hail my own, so I called a cab company while I was still at the interview site. I made three different calls waiting patiently after each one.

I don't know if the cab drove by and kept going or if the driver just never showed up, but whatever happened, I didn't get a cab. I had to schlep my two small girls three long blocks back to the hotel in the ice, snow, and cold. I must have looked like something out of a Charles Dickens novel pushing my way up Boston's city streets, a four-year-old toddler in one hand and carrying my one-year-old in another. It was a lonely, frustrating feeling and it was about that time I was thinking we might need to consider our other offer.

When we got back to the hotel, the girls were hungry. Howard wasn't back from his interview yet, so I decided to order up some room service for them. I dialed the number and tried to place my order, but the room service operator had other plans. It seems that the hotel was hosting a rather large wedding and in order to accommodate the wedding, they had suspended room service for the night. That was odd, but I pulled the girls together and called down to the restaurant. I hadn't really planned to go down there until Howard was back, but these were desperate times. I phoned down to the restaurant but they had not only suspended room service, they had shut down the entire restaurant. There I was in a strange city in the middle of winter, with two tired, hungry girls, unable to get a cab, and no place to get them something to eat. Although Boston is a fabulous city, with so much to do and see, we were not able to experience all it has to offer on that trip.

All I had to give the girls were M&Ms. You can only imagine what it was like giving a toddler all the M&Ms she can eat. Karelle got mashed M&Ms. To say the girls were bouncing off the walls is an understatement. As I searched the phonebook for places outside the hotel we could order from, Howard returned to the hotel and found out about our frustrating day. We were able to phone in an order from a surrounding restaurant and finally fill our growling bellies.

In contrast, our first experience with Cleveland was wonderful. It was an open, friendly city. At first thought, we assumed maybe it was because we had such a difficult time in Boston that Cleveland looked so good. The first person we met was the cab driver that picked us up from the airport and shuttled us to our temporary home at the Alcazar Hotel in Cleveland Heights. He was so welcoming and knowledgeable about the city. As we drove along, he would point out historical landmarks and other places of interest. In the end, we decided that Cleveland was the best place for us. People seemed forthcoming here in the Midwest.

Not long after, during our first Cleveland 4th of July celebration, we met a nice young couple at the festivities in Shaker Heights. We talked for a while, then much to Howard's and my surprise, we discovered that the renowned Dr. Jackson Wright and his beautiful wife Molly had been stationed in the same town as Howard's sister and her husband, and they were good friends! Of all the people who came out to see the fireworks, we were sitting right next to our new best friends. Imagine that!

Phyllis Hyman has always been my favorite artist of all time. I would have been so proud to have been able to sing like her, but I have learned to appreciate the talent I have been given and to give my best. One of the greatest moments of my life came when Howard and I were able to go backstage and meet Phyllis when she came to Cleveland for a performance. I happened to be friends with a school teacher, who had moved to the greater Cleveland area from Philadelphia. She had a daughter, who was a year older than my oldest daughter Ilea. They went to Lomond Elementary School together. She had been a childhood friend of Phyllis and her brother when they all lived in Philly. She knew that I loved the music of Phyllis Hyman and let me know that she and her brother were coming to town.

She gave Howard and me tickets and backstage passes. I was so elated that I had the florist send a bouquet of flowers to thank her. Before we all got into her black car the night of the performance, her brother said, "Phyllis wants us to bring her some soul food. Where can we get some in this town?" I directed them to the Nile Valley Restaurant just down the street. he asked, "Do they have greens? Phyllis said to be sure to get some greens." I assured him that they did. We picked up our order and headed straight downtown to Playhouse Square, the second largest theater district in the United States. We had fabulous seats and I was in heaven. Her brother had delivered the food to Phyllis before the performance and met us at our seats just before the show was about to begin.

Afterwards, we went backstage, ate from the trays of assorted meats, cheeses, fruits, and sliced veggies, and finally got to meet Phyllis in her dressing room. We all chatted a bit. I was silently saying to myself, *I cannot believe this is happening!* Howard, being the psychologist he is, showed Phyllis one of his mood assessment cards that changes color to show your mood when you hold your thumb on the square spot. Phyllis was so surprised to see that the card showed a green color which indicated she was calm. She got on her walkie-talkie with her attendants screaming to them that the card said she was calm. She was very excited about that! I got to sing and use sign language for one of Phyllis's newer releases "Don't Want to Change the World." She made a comment like, "Okay, girlfriend, tryin' to sing my song," in her no-nonsense attitude. We laughed.

Later that evening, we all left and went to the hotel where Phyllis was staying to visit with her a bit longer. By then she was taking off her make-up while she was lying in bed watching TV. She had just finished with one side of her face and was greasing up the other side in Vaseline when we arrived. She didn't seem to mind that we saw her without her make-up. We all talked some more and she sang some more, before it was time to go. Howard and I had a babysitter that was waiting. We all hugged her goodbye and I left on cloud nine!

It would be about six months or so after that experience that I would be stopped in my tracks with news on the radio that sadly announced Phyllis was dead. The tears began to stream down my face as I pulled into my garage. This wasn't just another artist who had succumbed to the demons many in the industry face, it was *my friend* Phyllis Hyman.

After years of living here, I can say that my first impressions of Cleveland were right. Many jokes have been made about this city, but if you've never been here, you can't know what a jewel it truly is. There is something here for everyone! It is such an accessible city with much to do from cultural events to nature walks and everything else in between. The Rock and Roll Hall of Fame is a popular attraction and our lakefront is going to be under development soon, making Cleveland an attractive destination city. With all of the great restaurants and chefs like Michael Simon, Cleveland is also becoming known as a foodie town. We have the second largest theater district in the country and the Gunnies Book of World Records has named Cleveland as having the largest outdoor chandelier right outside of Playhouse Square. Cleveland rocks!

Moving is always a hard thing to do. There is so much to take care of, not the least of which is finding a place to live. I had two small girls and a move to coordinate. The good thing about working for a hospital is that someone is always coming or going. Our luck had it that someone was going and they needed somebody to rent their house until it sold. The house sat directly in Richmond Heights, which was still very much in its development stage in the mid-1980s.

At the time, I wasn't working. During the day, it was just me and the girls existing alongside polite but distant neighbors. I felt the chasm acutely. I was also not prepared to find out less than a year after our arrival, six months to be exact, that the people whose house we rented from had sold it. We had almost no time at all to get out and get into our own place. In addition, we were still waiting for the condo in Pennsylvania to sell.

Again, one of Howard's colleagues at the hospital told us of a house next door to her that was for sale. The house was on a road called Ingleside, which is a long street that winds through both parts of Shaker Heights. There are two parts to Ingleside, one that rubs elbows with the larger city of Cleveland. The houses run toward the bungalow, built close together and lawns nicely tended. Then there is the other side of Ingleside where the houses tend to be a little larger, the lawns look professionally manicured, and the houses are a little further separated.

At the time I didn't know this about the inner ring suburbs of Cleveland. So when Howard's colleague suggested we look at houses for sale on her street I simply gave the realtor the name of the street and told him I wanted to see the house that was for sale. Now, here's where I thought the realtor might have been more helpful. When I gave him the street name it would have been nice if he had said to me that there was more than one house for sale on this street. But he didn't do that. He steered me right to the one bumping against the city.

Now, I have nothing against living near the city. Nothing bad was happening there. My life was never in danger. Our nights were not rattled with the sound of gunfire. But if I had had options, I would have liked to have known about them. Plus, that wasn't necessarily the house I was asking to see. Still, we bought it (false pretenses notwithstanding) and we had 12 good years in that house.

The day we moved in, I noticed a little girl sitting on the porch of the house two doors down. As the only child of Deaf parents, I never had the privilege of shyness. I went right up to the edge of her drive and asked, "Is your mommy home?" She said nothing and ran into the house. I think I scared her a bit with my forwardness at first. But little Tamika's mother, Tammy, and I became the best of friends later on. Tamika and my daughters also became good friends. Tamika would later become like another daughter to Howard and me. She was just one year older than Ilea. Tammy was one of my saving graces when I started my PhD program.

I got a job as an adjunct at Cleveland State University, teaching American Sign Language. I was pretty happy there. It was a part-time position; my girls were small and it gave me time to be with them while Howard worked the bear schedule. If I ever thought that getting a bachelor's and then a master's degree was beyond anything I could have conceived of, it was time to hold on to my hat. A dean from Cleveland State University gave me a call one evening and said, "Good evening, are you busy?"

When the dean calls, of course you are not busy.

"Cleveland State is in the second year of offering its PhD program in urban education. There is financial assistance available, I think you should apply," he stated with deliberateness.

Well after I picked my mouth up from the floor, I thanked him profusely for thinking of me. I did apply, got accepted, and before I even knew what was happening, I was working on my doctorate.

I had far exceeded my own expectations of myself let alone what others thought I could actually do. Of course, Howard just saw this as a natural progression of things. I was still having difficulty seeing myself as anything other than little Jeanie from Dover.

Now I had to take classes, teach, and take care of my two small girls and a husband! On the outside, my life must have looked positively chaotic! But I had good friends and a solid family structure that allowed us to be able to weather that process.

We also had the East China Restaurant. We lived on Chinese take-out and the kindness of my good friends, Tammy Perry (who has since passed through transition) and Rita. Let's face it, I was dedicated to my family, but a woman can only do so much. Something had to give and for me most of the time it was cooking. Teaching during the day and taking classes at night left very little time for the traditional meal or meal time.

Tammy had moved into a basement apartment on the edge of Shaker Heights. Two nights a week I would pick up the girls after school and take them directly to Tammy's and she'd hang on to them while I went to my class until Howard could get them when he came home from work in the evening.

I also had Rita, a Lebanese friend whose daughter was the same age as Ilea. I dropped off her daughter at school with my own daughters every morning. In the evening, two or three days a week, Rita returned the favor by cooking dinner for my family. She was such a good cook, she could have opened her own restaurant. She would fix falafel, tabbouleh, and other Lebanese delicacies that, at the time, I had never heard of.

Kim, another good friend, became the leader of our local Girl Scout troupe. I met her when she and I would take our daughters to Shaker Day School. Both girls became Daisies, Brownies, and ultimately, Girl Scouts. We also attended the same church where Kim and I were involved with the children's choir. Kim was (and still is) an excellent seamstress. During one of our Kwanzaa celebrations, she made stunning African outfits for our daughters to wear in the children's program.

Life is hard enough. Nobody should try it without good friends. I don't know what we would have done without those people in our lives at that time. I was far from my roots, my father was gone, and we were trying to make our way alone in a new city. That can be the loneliest time in a person's life, even with immediate family 4 hours or so away in Cincinnati.

Our house was always cluttered with somebody's school books, mine or the girls'. It was noisy and busy and full of life. Howard's hours were often brutal. But we always made time for the girls.

I dropped Karelle off at Shaker Day School, a preschool, with her amazing teachers, and Ilea at Lomond Elementary School in the morning with her beloved teachers. I made sure I was home in time and could pick them up when they got out of school in the afternoon. I suspect they had no idea the movement that took place between the time they left for school and the time they got back. But Howard and I made sure that we were there for every school function and parent teacher conference.

Where We Are Now

JAY-Z REITERATED THE LITTLE ORPHAN ANNIE ANTHEM that "it's a hard knock life." To some it can seem so. To others, it can be viewed as an opportunity of a lifetime.

The world can be an unkind place if you think it is and it can be a fabulous quest if you think it is. Either way you will be absolutely correct. Paths wind and twist and have a funny way of dropping you off in places you never thought you'd be. How you perceive where you are is a matter of choice. I choose to see it as an adventure!

I received my PhD in 1994 and worked at Cleveland State University until I applied and began working at Cuyahoga Community College in 1999. Currently, I am a tenured professor in the Liberal Arts Division in the American Sign Language and Deaf Interpretive Services Program, a two-and-a-half year program that teaches students how to become interpreters for people who are Deaf. I have the pleasure of working with a wonderful group of faculty, staff, students, and administrators who are dedicated to their profession. It is such a joy to come to work every day!

Howard has been at University Hospitals of Cleveland since we moved here in 1987 and has, over time, earned the title of Professor of Pediatrics, Psychiatry, and Psychological Sciences. He has established himself and is known in his profession as the grandfather of Psychoneuroimmunology. He sees patients as well as teaches residents. He is boarded in biofeedback and certified in biofeedback and hypnosis, and has been featured in many TV programs including one on deliberately caused bodily damage (DCBD), featured on the National Geographic Channel. His interest in this area is based on research he conducted in the Middle East on this phenomenon. In fact, when we have visited other countries, people have approached him saying, "Where do I know you from?" We laugh and then let them off the hook.

After I received my PhD, things settled down a bit. We moved into a roomier home—same city, different neighborhood. The girls found their own interests. Ilea chose the cello and ice skating, and Karelle chose the clarinet and horseback riding. Both girls had the opportunity to travel internationally while still in high school and Karelle in college as well.

In 2001, our family was so pleased to have been able to host our amazing foreign exchange student daughter from Australia, Laura Dillon Carson. To this day we have kept in contact with her and her lovely family Warrick, Gaye, Hannah, brother Nathan, husband Nathan, and their three beautiful children and a whole host of extended family members.

The girls have since graduated from college, Ilea with a bachelor's from Tennessee State University and a master's from Case Western Reserve University. Karelle graduated from Dartmouth College and is currently enrolled in a PhD program at Rutgers.

Karelle was featured and interviewed by Robin Roberts in the ABC News Special "The Reunion," a documentary about the planned integration of Shaker Heights. Shaker Heights, which I refer to as "The Garden of Eden of the Midwest," has been a superb city in which to live. We are a nationally and internationally known municipality continuing to strive for excellence in education, work, play, and relationships. Residing here is like living in a Thomas Kincaid painting. The sights and sounds of the flora and fauna are breathtaking anytime of the year.

My family and I also have had the opportunity to reconnect with my mother and begin a new dialog. It has given me a sense of peace and resolve in the idea that everything always works out for the best, even if it doesn't appear so when you're going through the tough times. We drove to Baltimore when my daughters were in their late twenties to pay her a visit.

It was during this time that I was able to ask her questions and to get answers from her perspective that would help me in the writing of this book. Currently, she and I chat occasionally via a relay service to see how things are going. It is a respectful relationship; however, it is not the deep connection I share with my own daughters. Nevertheless, we do communicate about generalities and the like.

Between the four of us, we have individually or collectively had the pleasure of traveling to many wondrous places on the planet such as Germany, Ireland, Belgium, New Zealand, Australia, Jordan, Egypt,

Karelle, Howard, me, and Ilea.

Puerto Rico, England, Amsterdam, France, Italy, Barbados, the Bahamas, Iraq, Kurdistan, Jamaica, Grand Cayman Islands, Haiti, Mexico, the U.S. Virgin Islands, St. Thomas, St. Maarten, Jerusalem, Poland, Aruba, and Benin, West Africa.

In 2000 I started the J. Paris Mosley Scholarship Foundation Fund (in the name of my father) with the Cleveland Foundation, the world's first community foundation and our nation's second largest community foundation. This fund provides scholarships to Deaf and hard-of-hearing high school seniors who need financial assistance to support their desire to attend college or to pursue other postsecondary options. Applications for the scholarship may be accessed at www.clevelandfoundation.org. We also started two family businesses Mosley's Shoe Cosmetics, LLC and HIJK International, LLC.

I'm sure that my dad would be so very proud of how we all turned out. Even though he is not physically here to witness his impact on the world through us, his presence is still felt. Sometimes, when no one is looking I look back on my path, see how far I have come and I want to be like Willow Smith and "whip my hair" in that carefree way that seems available only to nine-year-old girls. I want to dance until I fall and sing until my voice is gone. Sometimes I do.

AFTERWORD

I HOPE THAT YOU HAVE GARNERED THE MESSAGE THAT I have tried to demonstrate through the story of me and my dad's life. No matter where you come from, it is possible to get anywhere you want to go. Quieting the negative chatter in your head by focusing your mind via whatever manner you choose and changing your thoughts, you can change your life. Then, be prepared to do the work necessary to get you there. Have a passion for what it is that you want. That's not to say that there won't be obstacles. The key is to find a way to move past them. The multiverse is larger than any human barrier and can find ways to provide you with solutions. I have learned that it is important to include thoughts of love and gratitude for the things you have already been given, as that is how more will be given to you. Project an interest in and enthusiasm for life. People are more willing to help and support someone who is ready and eager to help themselves. The "woe is me" approach repels. When you are ready, the multiverse will provide people and circumstances to aid you in accomplishing your goals.

There is a saying, "When the student is ready, the teacher will appear." I would like to add that we should all remember, when that person does appear in your life to offer you assistance, don't just have your hand out to receive, but also think of ways you can return a gift. That person doesn't just appear in your life to give something to you. There is something that you can do for that person as well. It's reciprocal. It doesn't have to be grand; it could be as small as a smile and a thank you. Be creative. Think of how you can be a help to others. You can also be the teacher that appears in someone else's life. As Maya Angelou said, "Be a blessing." Pass it on. In the Christian tradition, we have a saying: Work like everything depends on you and pray like everything depends on God.

When things do not work out as you've planned, don't give up. Say "thank you for this opportunity to learn, because the multiverse has a better plan for me." Keep yourself in the game. Education is the key to getting anywhere in life. The more education you have, the more opportunities can appear. Believe that you can do it. Put action behind those beliefs, and acknowledge the gifts that will show up in your life by showing gratitude in whatever way you can. Receive a blessing, be a blessing. Saying thank you and giving back in some way not only helps others, but it also helps you to succeed even more. That's a win-win for everyone!

I hope that the telling of my dad's and my story will inspire you to, as I heard one radio personality say, "Make your mark on the world before your relevance becomes obsolete." We all can benefit from what you have to offer. Remember that we all share our resources on this planet with others, that we need to take care of it, and that we need to be kind to one another. When things in your life are not going as planned, don't give up on yourself or your dream. If you hold on, persevere, and have faith in yourself, you may find that things will turn out even better than you would have ever expected.

Growing up experiencing multiple cultures—African American, Native American, European American, hearing, deaf—has allowed me to see that there are far more things we have in common than those that would divide us. Everyone wants to be acknowledged, loved, and to be significant.

We are on this planet to serve one another with the talents and special gifts given to us by the Great Spirit, the Creator, God, or as the now famous neurosurgeon and author of *Proof of Heaven*, Dr. Eben Alexander has named this entity, OM. By whatever name we refer to this divine being, we are to use what we are given to uplift each other and to make this world a better place for everyone. If we can see ourselves in others, we would see how it's just our fear of the unknown that keeps us apart and keeps us from being our best.

In nature, the leaves on a tree can be of varying shades. Wouldn't it be silly for one leaf to criticize the other for being a darker or lighter shade of green, or for being a different color altogether? Each leaf belongs to the tree and receives nourishment from the same source.

E-wee-ne-tu, wummoi, ok ne moo ye-ow-wass! (Peace, love, and joy!)—Nanticoke

Dad in the garden.

ACKNOWLEDGMENTS

NO UNDERTAKING CAN BE DONE WITHOUT THE HELP OF others. To the many people who have assisted me in this labor of love, I offer my sincere thanks and appreciation. I am extremely grateful to each of you for your contribution to this work.

This memoir could not have been written without the understanding, and support of my family, my amazing husband Howard, and my two remarkable daughters, Ilea and Karelle. Howard, thank you for reading and providing commentary from the perspective of the reader. In addition to your support, your reactions to this writing and advice were priceless. Ilea, thank you for your encouragement and support to keep writing. Karelle, thank you for your support and assistance with the research and editorial comments needed to complete this memoir. I am so blessed to have you as my family.

I am forever indebted to my Aunt Grace Kemp for her patience enduring all of my questions for so many years. Without her stories, this memoir would not have been as colorful. I am so sorry that your passing preceded the publication of this memoir, but I know you are watching over it and me from above.

I would also like to thank, posthumously, my Aunt Alice Thomas for your tolerance in handling my barrage of inquiries and for sharing your stories that were so vital to this work.

A special thanks goes to my cousins Charles Durham (who has gone through transition before the publication of this memoir) and Ronald Smith for your willingness to fill in the gaps. The information you shared with me allowed me to better understand the details of my family's life that occurred before I was born.

I want to especially thank Gayle Williamson for your unique talent in pulling together the myriad of loose ends of a story into a cohesive and pleasurable reading experience. Because you were willing to help me from the very beginning, your friendship has been invaluable.

Al Nola's guidance on the technical aspects of shoe repair machinery was extremely helpful. You took the time out of your busy schedule at Al Nola's Shoe Repair to walk me through your shop explaining each detail about the machines that help deliver such a great product. Al, your work is the best!

Thank you to the outstanding staff at Moto Photo in Shaker Heights for all your help in making sure my photos for this memoir were of the highest quality.

I am most grateful to Mrs. Helen Hicks for the information you were able to provide about Booker T. Washington Elementary School. Information regarding the process of delivering students to their teachers and other details were much appreciated.

I am deeply indebted to my friends Jacqueline Renee Brown, Wilma Harris Chapman, and Cynthia Edmonds Martin for your contributions. You were instrumental in providing names, places, and dates that I had forgotten. I also would like to thank you for your memories and for being such good lifelong friends.

There are several others to whom I would like to express my gratitude for reading my manuscript and providing vital feedback. Ms. Ivey Pittle Wallace, Ms. Melissa Mathews, and Ms. Deirdre Mullervy at Gallaudet University Press provided numerous comments central to the completion of this memoir. Your critical eye and analysis of how my manuscript could be improved is just what was needed to make this document cohesive and clear. Thank you to the entire team!

Susanna DeSorgo's assessment proved to be invaluable. Not knowing the story prior to reading the manuscript and being able to read it from a detached perspective gave me the veridical feedback so necessary for an objective critique. Thank you for your expertise and friendship.

A thank you to my sister-in-law, Lillian Hawkins, for your support in the writing of this story. As a published author, I deeply value your opinion.

This book could not have been written without the assistance of Sterling Street from the Nanticoke Indian Museum, and my cousins Doris Price, her sister Sylvia Pinkett, and their brother William Davis of the Nanticoke Indian Association, Inc. Your eagerness and enthusiasm in sharing with me your priceless knowledge about our ancestry and the history and life of the Nanticoke people is much appreciated. You were so critical to the completion of this work.

Chief Natosha Norwood Carmine of the Nanticoke Indian Tribe, thank you for your progressive thinking, support, and willingness to provide your valued comments. You represent the positive future of our tribe. Thank you for all you do!

I would like to offer many thanks to the renowned Dr. Charles Johnson for being willing to assist me in taking this manuscript to the next level. Being the accomplished, award-winning author that you are and taking the time out of your very busy schedule to help guide me throughout this process speaks volumes about your humbleness and generosity. Your words of wisdom were invaluable in helping me to complete this account of my dad's and my life story.

My family and I have been truly blessed by so many of you. There are countless others that have enriched our lives who are too numerous to name. Again, we thank you! Peace and blessings upon each and every one of you.

REFERENCES

Anderson, Glenn B., and Katrina R. Miller. 2004. "In Their Own Words: Researching Stories About the Lives of Deaf People of Color." *Multicultural Perspectives* 6(2): 28–33.

Audicus. 2014. "Before American Sign Language, There Was Native American Sign Language." http://www.audicus.com.

Berke, Jamie. Resources and Information for Deaf Native Americans: American Indians with hearing loss. [Online] Available http://www .verywell.com, June 19, 2017.

Big Orrin. 2017. "Nanticoke Indian Fact Sheet." http://bigorrin.org /nanticoke_kids.htm.

Center on Disability Studies. 2017. "Walking between Two Worlds: Deaf Native American Identity and Accessibility Issues." http://www .pacrim.hawaii.edu.

Davis, Jeffrey E. 2010. *Hand Talk: Sign Language among American Indian Nations*. New York: Cambridge University Press.

DuBois, W.E.B. 1989. *The Souls of Black Folk*. New York: Bantam Books.

Ganondagan. "What is Wampum?" Accessed September 16, 2017. http:// www.ganondagan.org.

Gellert, Kapuaolaokalaniakea, William Hal Martin, Jodi A. Lapidus, Leslie Wosnig, and Thomas M. Becker. 2017. "Hearing-Related Health among Adult American Indians from a Pacific Northwest Tribe." *American Journal of Preventive Medicine* 52(3): S258–S262.

Hairston, Ernest, and Linwood Smith. 1983. *Black and Deaf in America: Are We That Different*. Silver Spring, MD: T.J. Publishers.

Hofsinde, Robert. 1956. *Indian Sign Language*. New York: Morrow.

Hunter, L. L., C. S. Davey, A. Kohtz, and K. A. Daly. 2007. "Hearing Screening and Middle Ear Measures in American Indian Infants and

Toddlers." *International Journal of Pediatric Otorhinolaryngology* 71:1429–38.

Jennings, Julianne. "The Silent Ones: Indians and Hearing Loss." https://indiancountrymedianetwork.com/news/opinions/the-silent-ones-indians-and-hearing-loss.

Legay, Gilbert. 2007. *Dictionary of North American Indians and Other Indigenous Peoples*. New York: Barron's.

Mallery, Garrick. 1881. *Sign Language among North American Indians Compared with that among Other Peoples and Deaf-Mutes*. Washington, DC: Smithsonian Institution Bureau of American Ethnology.

McCaskill, Carolyn, Ceil Lucas, Robert Bayley, and Joseph Hill. 2011. *The Hidden Treasure of Black ASL: Its History and Structure*. Washington, DC: Gallaudet University Press.

Murray, William V. 1996. *A Vocabulary of the Nanticoke Dialect*. Southhampton, PA: Evolution.

Nanticoke Indian Heritage Project. *A Photographic Survey of the Indian River Community*. Millsboro, DE: Indian Mission Church, 1977. Available from https://archives.delaware.gov/wp-content/.../PhotoSurveyIndianRiverCommunity.pdf.

Nanticoke Indian Tribe. "History." http://www.nanticokeindians.org.

Native-Languages. "Native Languages of the Americas: Nanticoke (Southern Delaware)." http://www.native-languages.org/nanticoke.htm.

Native-Languages. "Vocabulary in Native American Languages: Nanticoke Words." http://www.native-languages.org/nanticoke_words.htm.

Oldfather, Dustin and Mariya. "Nanticoke Traditions Still Run Deep in Southern Delaware." http://www.capegazette.com/affiliate-post/nanticoke-traditions-still-run-deep-southern-delaware/123909.

Onondaga Nation People of the Hills. "Wampum." http://www.onondaganation.org.

Paris, Damora Goff, and Sharon Kay Wood. 2002. *Step Into The Circle: The Heartbeat of American Indian, Alaska Native, and First Nations Deaf Communities*. Salem, OR: AGO.

Paris, Damora Goff, Sharon Kay Wood, & Katrina Miller. 2002. A brief overview of the contributions of AISL to ASL. In D. G. Paris, S. K. Wood, & K. Miller (Ed.), *Step Into The Circle: The Heartbeat of*

American Indian, Alaska Native, and First Nations Deaf Communities (pp. 37–41). Salem, OR: AGO.

Porter, Frank W. 1987. *The Indians of North America: The Nanticoke.* New York: Chelsea House.

Pritzker, Barry M. 2000. *A Native American Encyclopedia: History, Culture and Peoples.* New York: Oxford University Press.

Sacred Circle. "Sacred Circle." http://www.deafnative.com.

Seton, Ernest Thompson. 1918. *Sign Talk of the Cheyenne Indians and Other Cultures.* New York: Dover.

Terry, Betty, and Raymond Mitsawokett: "A 17th Century Native American Community in Delaware." http://www.nativeamericansof-delawarestate.com.

Ulen, Eisa. "The Double Divide: Deaf and Native." http://indiancountry-medianetwork.com.

Weslager, C. A. 2006. *Delaware's Forgotten Folk: The Story of the Moors & Nanticokes.* Philadelphia: University of Pennsylvania Press.

Weslager, C. A. 1983. *The Nanticoke Indians: Past and Present.* Newark: University of Delaware Press.

Wurtzburg, S., and L. Campbell. 1995. "North American Indian sign language: Evidence of its existence before European contact." *International Journal of American Linguistics*, 61(2), 153–167.